W9-APH-387

SO YOU WANT TO BE A LAWYER?

A Guide to success in the Legal Profession

By

MARIANNE PILGRIM CALABRESE
And
SUSANNE MARY CALABRESE

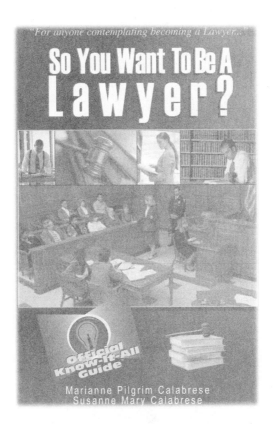

"For anyone contemplating becoming a Lawyer..."

So You Want To Be A
Lawyer?

Official Know-it-All Guide

Marianne Pilgrim Calabrese
Susanne Mary Calabrese

Dedication

Now, as always, to all our friends and family who have helped us throughout this process.
And "To mothers and daughters' everywhere who love and help each other.

"For anyone contemplating becoming a Lawyer..."

So You Want To Be A
Lawyer?

Official
Know-It-All
Guide

Marianne Pilgrim Calabrese
Susanne Mary Calabrese

Table of Content

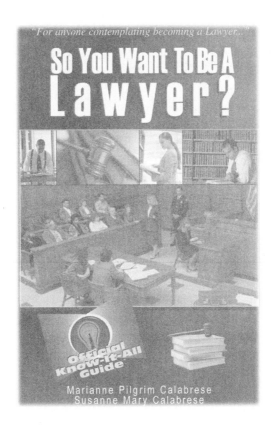

"For anyone contemplating becoming a Lawyer...

So You Want To Be A
Lawyer?

Official Know-It-All Guide

Marianne Pilgrim Calabrese
Susanne Mary Calabrese

Acknowledgements

Marianne's Acknowledgements

I would like to give special thanks to Ron Davidson who helped immensely with the work on, So You Want To Be A Lawyer?.
To my friends and family Robert Albano, Virgina and Verity Bostick, John Calabrese III, Yolanda and Dave Carriero, Peggy and Steve Carriero, Sherry Cole, Debbie Collins, Kathleen Conway-Gervais, Ann and Dan Davidson, Sue Hoffman, Theresa Munz, Linda and Kevin Murtagh, and Francine Pilgrim, who all gave us exceptional help, love and encouragement.

Special acknowledgement to, Christine M. Stevenson, the lawyer who gave outstanding advice in making this book and to all the lawyers who helped make this book possible.

Susanne's Acknowledgement's

I would like to thank all of the wonderful legal professionals I have worked with who have taken the time to speak with me and impart their knowledge of the profession. I would also like to thank all my friends and family; especially my father, John Calabrese, who has supported me throughout my own career search, my brother John Calabrese III, my best friend Heather Filippi and my traveling companion Domenic Alonge.

In particular, I would also like to thank John and David Reilly, who gave me my first position in the legal field and whose kindness I will always remember. Also to Peter McIsaac, Andras Teleki, Rachael Zufall, Jacqueline Evans and Wendy Quandahl who taught me everything I know. And to Deborah Meyers, Eugene Licker, Susanna Auyeung, Matthew Trotter, and John Adler who are all the most amazing and supportive people one could hope to work with.

Scope, Plan and Purpose

So You Want to Be A Lawyer? is a book for anyone who is or who wants to be a lawyer. The book reveals everything nobody else will tell you about the legal profession. It shows how to save the agony of on the job trial and error training and gives you a head start in using experienced strategies while dealing with partners, colleagues and clients. It doesn't teach you about the law, it enlightens you about the different aspects of a legal career. It tells you what type of law will be best for you and where to find your right position. There are The Ten Commandments of a Lawyer, which sums up in ten steps how to survive in the legal profession and gives in depth reasons why the Ten Commandments work.

This book is a refreshingly new and realistic look at the reality that lawyers may not succeed in a law firm because of their interactions with partners, colleagues and clients and not because they don't know the law.

The chapter topics are;

1. Why do you want to be a lawyer?
2. Law School and the Bar Exam
3. Law Practice Environments
4. Types of law
5. Meet the lawyers
6. Salaries and Opportunities
7. Partners and Colleagues
8. How to Deal with Clients, Colleagues, and Paralegal staff
9. Making the Firm Work For You,
10. The Ten Commandments of a Lawyer

Each of these topics are discussed fully with real life stories and examples. There are easy steps given on how to handle each issue and how a lawyer can ease into a law firm. The Ten Commandments make it easy for you to sum up the dos and don'ts to survive in the legal profession.

Preface

So You Want To Be A Lawyer? Is a realistic way of looking at a lawyer's role and tells you what no one else will tell you about the legal profession. Entertaining narrative stories are incorporated into the text to give the reader first hand knowledge of real life situations. These authentic tales show how lawyers behave and interact with colleagues, partners, clients and how one can best handle each situation. The Ten Commandments of a Lawyer provides as a guide to success in easing into any law situation and is a summary of the main ideas from the book.

Anyone interested in a career in the law profession and how to survive in it will find this book both worthwhile and entertaining reading. It is a must read for anyone who wants to be a lawyer, who is a lawyer, has just started their career as a lawyer, or who is in law school. *So You Want To Be A Lawyer?* Lays out in detail all the career options available to an attorney and it will be very influential in the decision making of anyone who is considering becoming a lawyer or contemplating a change of careers. This book gives a new outlook on life in the law profession.

Introduction

So You Want To Be A Lawyer? shows you ways to ease into any law situation with partners, colleagues, clients, paralegal and legal secretaries and gives you helpful hints through, The Ten Commandments of a Lawyer and by using entertaining real life narratives.

Chapter 1 : Why Do You Want To Be A Lawyer?
* Why do you want to be a lawyer?
* How to determine your own success
* Find out what you expect from a law career
* Find your strengths and weaknesses to achieve your goals
* How to balance your life

In this chapter you will explore the reasons why you want to go into the legal profession. Questions are presented that will help you decide if law is the right career for you. Insights into the legal profession and what position will be best for you are discussed.

This chapter gives realistic insights into your personal expectations, goals, values and needs. It helps you find your strengths and weaknesses and enables you to realize whether a career in law will bring you the type of success you want as well as a balance to your life.

Chapter 2: "Law School and the Bar Exam"
* How to get into law school
* What would be the best law school for you
* Financing your legal education
* What to expect when you get into law school
* What to do if you don't get into law school
* The Bar Exam

This chapter tells you how to get into the best law school for you. It gives you three basic hints on how to apply to law school. Topics of discussion include academic records, LSAT scores, finances and how to use these to better your chances of getting into law school. Questions such as, "What can I do if I didn't do well on the LSAT?" are answered.

This chapter helps you realize what things are most important to you when applying to law school. Factors such as environment, faculty, and special programs, are analyzed. It enlightens you on how to proceed and what to do after you are accepted to law school and also what to do if you are not.

Chapter 3: Law Practice Environment
* History of Law
* Private Practice
* Large, medium and small firms
* Corporation lawyers
* Government positions
* Solo Practice

Chapter 3 will give you a realistic view of the different law environments and which will be the best for you to work in. It tells you what you always wanted to know about private practice, large, medium and small law firms, corporations and government positions. It gives you helpful hints on when to leave a position and which to use as a stepping stone to get to your ultimate goal position. It tells you what each law environment can provide and how to work in it for your best success.

Chapter 4: "Types of Law"
* Roles of lawyers
* Forms of Practice
* Business Law, Criminal Law, Tort Law, Family Practice, Elder Law, Property Law, Public Interest Law, Labor Law, Employment Law, Work Place Law, Intellectual Property Law, Environmental Law, Health Law, Immigration Law, International Law, Tax Attorney and Boutique Areas.

This chapter will introduce you to the different roles of lawyers within the various types of law. It will help you find what role you are best suited for - whether it is advisor or litigator.

You will learn the different forms of practice from transactional to educational and how you will fit into each. Analyzing the different types of law from Business to International will help you key into the type of law you are most interested and suited for.

Chapter 5: Meet the Lawyers
*   Analyzing lawyer's personalities
*   Do The Right Thing Lawyer, High Income Lawyer, Solo Practitioner
*   Lawyer, Make a Difference Lawyer, Back to Roots Lawyer, and
    Engineer Turned Lawyer, the Never Can Please Lawyer, and the
    Royalty Lawyer.

This chapter reveals the typical lawyer personalities you will encounter when you become a lawyer. Examples from the most caring lawyer to the lawyer who only is concerned with money will be depicted. It will give you insights into the personalities you will encounter and how this knowledge can help you succeed to become the lawyer that you want to be.

Many types of lawyers are described. Bill is a criminal lawyer who wants to make sure people who are a threat to society get locked up for a good long time. Sam is a high income tax lawyer who works for a large law firm. Maggie who opened her own successful law practice started from nothing and grew into a successful lawyer. Jeff is a passionate lawyer who feels he helps and makes a difference in his company. Marie, after graduating law school, went back to her old neighborhood to help the community. Jane is an employment lawyer who works with good people who have been wronged knowing she is going to do something for them. Jim, the engineer who turned into a Patent Lawyer became very successful both financially and personally. Jean is a lawyer who is difficult to work with, but is highly dedicated to her firm. Charles is an attorney who needs work done his own way and is catered to within the firm.

Chapter 6: Salaries and Opportunities
*   How and where to find a law position
*   Where future law positions will be
*   Best areas to seek law positions
*   Opportunities in large, medium and small cities,
    towns and rural areas
*   What to do if you can't find a position
*   Hints on how to make yourself more marketable
*   Salaries, billable hours and contingencies
        In this chapter the hard facts are given about salaries and

opportunities of lawyers seeking a position. You are given four factors in finding a position. You will learn where the future law position will be and the best areas to practice in. This chapter will tell you how to better market yourself and how to find the best law position to satisfy your most important priorities.

Chapter 7: Partners and Colleagues
*   Hierarchical structure
*   Partners, the most important people in the firm
*   How to work with partners
*   Generation gap and how to work in it
*   Unsupervised, supervisory and supervised work
*   How to achieve your goals

   This chapter will give you the hierarchical structure of most law firms and tell you who the most important people are and why. It also tells you how and why to handle the important partners in order to succeed in the firm. It acquaints you with the working order and how to recognize the pecking order and the way to succeed in it. It will explain the powers of the equity partner, managing partner, general partners, and junior partners. Of counsel, senior associates, summer associates, staff attorneys and how they can affect you and your position will also be discussed. It will answer questions on how to work for a difficult equity partner, and what you should do as a junior associate when working with partners.

Chapter 8: How to Deal With Clients, Colleagues and Paralegal staff
*   Relationships between you and the client
*   How to work with colleagues and partners
*   Firms polices
*   When to change your position
*   How to work with paralegal staff and legal secretaries

   This chapter will give you valuable information on how to deal with clients, colleagues, partners and paralegal to insure your success. It will give you helpful hints on how to deal with difficult colleagues especially partners and how to work with them within the firm's policies.

Chapter 9: Make the Law Firm Work for You
* Conforming to the firm's procedures
* How to successfully enter the best group for you
* Techniques to successfully work with colleagues and clients.
* Find out if you are optimistic or pessimistic and make it work for you
* Insights into your own coping skills
* Balance in your life

This chapter will enable you to successfully have the firm work for you. It will explain many strategies that will help you know how and what to do in order to get the most from the firm. You will learn how and when to conform to the firms procedures and norms. It will explain how to identify and meet group expectation in order to enter the best group for you. You will find out whether you are more pessimistic or optimistic and how to have these traits work for you.

You will learn how to make your own opportunities in the firm with self-awareness, networking and positioning. You are also given insights into your coping mechanisms such as avoidance, procrastination, disorganization and others to find out if they are working for you. The end result is a balanced life that you created with the cooperation of the firm working for you.

Chapter 10 The Ten Commandments of A Lawyer
1. Work for partners who like you
2. Balance your personal and professional life
3. Don't alienate any clients
4. Work for the right size and type firm for your goals
5. Work In the area of law you find interesting
6. Utilizes legal secretaries and paralegals effectively and respectfully
7. Follow established polices and procedures of the firm
8. Always have a professional attitude
9. Bill hours to clients effectively
10. Don't alienate any colleagues

This chapter gives details on how to fulfill the Ten Commandments of a Lawyer in order to achieve a successful entry into the legal profession.

Chapter One

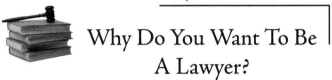

Why Do You Want To Be A Lawyer?

Why do you want to be lawyer? That is the major question you should answer before you start a career in law. Do you want to be a lawyer to help society, to make a difference to a certain group or to make a lot of money? What are your reasons for wanting to become a lawyer? Becoming a lawyer is a major decision. Before deciding, make sure you have all the facts so you can make an educated choice if the legal profession is really for you. This book helps you do that.

Law is a more demanding profession then most people realize. It is not the Perry Mason kind of career portrayed on television. It is also not the high-income profession that most people think it is. There are some attorneys that earn a lot of money but there are also many attorneys who just about make a living. You must also keep in mind that there are more lawyers then there are jobs so you will not be guaranteed your dream position when you graduate. You will be able to find some kind of position in the law field if you are versatile. A person who is content with his current career should not seek out a law degree simply to improve his economic standing.

How you define success is an individual preference. Is it helping people, making money, becoming an indispensable team player? Is it working 8AM to 5 PM five days a week, going home with no further thoughts about your work? Or is it thoroughly having your job be your life? Is it working in a law firm in a corporate section, big firm or small firm, or your own firm? Or is success working within a particular type of law? It is important to take the time and determine your definition of success. One thing is clear, in order to succeed you have to take control of your career. Since job satisfaction plays an important role in whether success is achieved you must take steps to ensure your own happiness

Choosing a career is about being able to make careful decisions in an analytical process. Your job will be to analyze the pros and cons of a law career, taking into consideration things such as how much you will be paid, how much education you will need, where you will have to live or relocate to, what type of law you may have to specialize in and what kind of setting you want and can find work in. A career in law is absolutely dependent on solid analytical skills. According to the oath you will take after you pass your state bar exam you are required to do everything ethically possible to represent the interests of your client within the bounds of the law.

If you like dealing with people and helping them, law can be a great profession for you. Law can give you the skills to protect the minority community, counsel women on their rights in a domestic dispute, draft new laws to preserve the ozone layer, assure the accused of their constitutional rights, devise corporate structures to facilitate the acquisition of new businesses, or teach others about consumer affairs. You can assist political candidates with their positions on key social legal issues, fight to protect the rights of the elderly in institutional care, assist parents with property issues, raise capital to fund an inventor's idea, correct the wrong done by an unsafe product, or help with taxes.

Think very carefully about a career in law before you start. If you haven't worked in a law firm in some capacity you may want to do so before you decide to pursue a career in law. Working in a law firm may be very different than what you expected and different types of law firms or law departments will have various types of working environments. It is advisable to work, volunteer or even interview lawyers from at least two or three different firms and practice areas before you commit yourself to a career in law. First-hand experience is always the best way to learn if a career is right for you. You may want to find summer employment at a law firm. Often smaller law firms will take on legal clerks or legal assistants during the summer when many attorneys and full-time employees take their vacations. Looking through the employment ads and asking family and friends is always one way of finding these positions. Most law firms also use employment agencies, or headhunters to fill critical positions.

Applying to placement agencies that specialize in attorneys is often a quick and effective way of finding a position in law.

If you do not have the luxury of working or volunteering at a law firm, interviewing attorneys is a rather time-efficient and extremely beneficial way of discovering whether law is the right career for you. If you have any family or friends that are practicing attorneys, set up a time to talk with them about their career. Even if you have a general knowledge of what this person's career entails, asking them specifically about your personal expectations often uncovers insight that you have never considered before.

Another excellent resource for finding information is contacting the alumni relations' office at the college or university you attended. This office most likely keeps records of alumni from your school that are attorneys practicing in your area. Some schools even have specific lists of people who have volunteered to help career counsel other alumni in law. These alumni often have wonderful insight, advice on how to learn more about a law career, stories of their past experiences and sometimes they even have tips on where to find job opportunities. A call to the alumni office is quick and easy – and definitely worth the effort.

Soul-searching is Difficult – A Quiz to Help

After any interviews or job opportunities you have, the ultimate decision is all about you – what YOU want out of your career. Knowing what your expectations are and then comparing them to the realities of the legal profession will help you make an educated decision.

Before you can make a decision you must become in tuned with your needs, goals, strengths and weakness. Answer the following questions and note your answers. These questions will help you evaluate why you want to become a lawyer.

1. How large a part of wanting to be a lawyer is your desire to help people?
2. How important is salary to your desire to be a lawyer?
3. How important is job security to you?
4. Are you willing to commit a lot of time and money to education and training?
5. What kind of setting do you want to work in?

6. How much stress can you handle on the job?

7. Do you want to be your own boss, run a business in partnership with others, or will you be content as a salaried employee?

8. How well do you deal with authority figures?

9. Can you pay attention to detail, handle paper work, legal documents and reports?

10.Are you a good writer, litigator, counselor, researcher and consultant?

By completing this exercise and writing your answers down, you now have more clear and focused career expectations that you can use throughout this book. If you decide law is for you, keep your initial goals in mind during the subsequent chapters when deciding what type of firm or company you would like to work for, what type of law you would like to practice and what type of opportunities you would like to pursue. Below is a discussion of each of the questions posed above and a discussion of how each issue comes to play in the law field.

(1) The Legal profession is a service industry. Helping people, groups or corporations is an important factor in being a lawyer. If you only go into law for the money you may be very disappointed. You may land the lawyers position of your dreams and always have it or you may not find a job as a lawyer and do something related to law. (Refer to Chapter 4: Types of Law for more information about different career choices.)

(2) Not all lawyers make a lot of money. In fact, most of the large paychecks are found in corporate practice fields, corporate law, mergers/acquisitions, corporate finance, tax, or working in house for a corporation. If you would like a career in public service, the paychecks are significantly lower than if you worked in a corporate practice field or a large law firm. Also, many sacrifices come with a large paycheck such as enormous work hours, strenuous caseloads and intense stress to perform. Often lawyers are not even able to enjoy their paycheck for many years because most of it will go to paying back student loans. (Refer to Chapter 6: Salaries and Opportunities for more information.)

(3) There are more lawyers than there are law positions. So you may have to put some time and effort into finding a position and then you may have to take a position you are not really interested in just to get started. . (Refer to Chapter 6: Salaries and Opportunities for more information.)

(4) Three to four years of your life, tens of thousands of dollars and a million headaches will be required to get your law degree. It can be an enormously worthwhile process, or a big mistake. Make sure you do the research, seriously think about your goals, understand the huge commitment and read this book   carefully before making this decision. (Refer to Chapter 4 :Types of Law)

(5) A law career provides you with so many opportunities for work settings. You may be able to find a position in any setting that suits your needs. (Refer to Chapter 5 : Meet the Lawyers)

(6) Any position can be stressful but depending on what type of law you go into the stress level can be more then the average job. (Refer to Chapter 8 : How to Deal with Clients, Colleagues, Partners and Paralegal staff)

(7) You may become your own boss if you are willing to put in the lean hard long years in order to get established, but you also may be a salaried employee for many years. (Refer to Chapter 7 : Partners and Colleagues)

(8) Who your clients are and the partners of the law firm are going to be your authority figures. You are going to have to have a good repose with them in order to succeed as a lawyer. (Refer to Chapter 6 : Salaries and Opportunities and Chapter 8: How to Deal With Clients, Colleagues and Paralegal Staff)

(9) Handling detail is inevitably a large part of becoming a lawyer. Keep this in mind when making your decision. (Refer to Chapter 4: Types of Law)

(10) Do you think you have the skills to be a lawyer? A special gift or talent can be shared in a very powerful way in a legal career, but sometimes it takes more than talent to succeed in the legal profession. Follow Chapter 10: The Ten Commandments of a Lawyer to learn how to survive and succeed in the legal profession.

A law career can bring you satisfaction, intellectual stimulation and a reasonable income. You will face new issues each day, meet new people with new problems. It will not be boring because you have the flexibility to change what you are doing and use your training on something that does interest you. This is a wonderful ability to have and the law provides this. So evaluate these questions and your answers and keep them in mind as you read this book. They will help you decide if law is the right career for you.

Your Strengths and Weaknesses

Once you know what you want and why, you then have to look at your strengths and weaknesses in order to achieve your goals. You also have to look at the threats and opportunities that come to you from the outside. When strengths, weaknesses, opportunities and threats are identified then you can determine your goal plan. Before reacting to an opportunity or a threat you have to understand your own strengths and weaknesses.

Your strengths are those skills that you perform better than your peers or colleagues. What are you especially good at? What comes easy to you and what do you do well? Make a list of your strengths. Are you are good writer, public speaker, negotiator etc. These strengths will determine many things about your career such as the type of law you want to go into and how you get there.

Knowing your weaknesses is almost as important as knowing your strengths. It is not easy to state your weaknesses, but it is important to come to terms with them. They are usually the things you don't like to do. Some weaknesses you can change others you won't be able to, but must work around. Some you will be able to train to become your strengths in order to do your job .You do need to know those areas that can hold you back and what you can do about it. Make a list of what you feel are your weaknesses and what if anything you can do about them.

The main thing about opportunities and threats is to be able to recognize them and to react in a way that will bring your success. Some threats and opportunities are in your control while others are not. What is outside your control can lessen your chances of success. Concentrate on what you do have control over and use that for your success.

Here are a few questions you can ask yourself:

1. Are you using all your strengths?
2. Why are you living with your weaknesses? Can you improve them?
3. What can you do to minimize potential threats to your career?
4. What are you doing to maximize your potential opportunities?
5. Are your goals realistic?

Now think back to your goals and purpose. How can your strengths, weaknesses, opportunities and threats effect you goals? For example if you want to be a criminal lawyer then hopefully one of your strengths is public speaking. If not you might have to change your goal or work on changing your public speaking skills.

Definition of a Lawyer

A Lawyer is defined by his or her commitment to the peaceful resolution of disputes. Lawyers act as both advocates and advisors in our society. As advocates, they represent one of the opposing parties in criminal and civil actions by presenting evidence that support their client's case. As advisors they counsel their clients as to their legal rights and obligations and suggest particular courses of action in business and personal matters. Whether acting as advocates or advisors, all attorneys interpret the law and apply it to specific situations. This requires knowledge, interpretative and communication evaluation skills, research and writing abilities and negotiation and persuasive talents.

There are many facets of the job you will need to master when and if you decide to be a lawyer. You are agreeing to represent clients by provided them with an informal understanding of their legal rights and obligations. As advocate, a lawyer asserts the client's position under the rules of the adversary system. As negotiator, a lawyer tries to settle advantageously for the client. As intermediary between clients, a lawyer tries to reconcile their difference in a fair manner. A lawyer acts as an evaluator when examining a client's legal affairs. A lawyer keeps information confidential except when disclosure is required by the Rules of Professional Conduct. (A copy of the Rules of Professional Conduct for your state may be found on the American Bar Association's WebPages, www.abanet.org.)

A lawyer's conduct should abide by the law both professional and personally. Lawyers should use the legal process only for legitimate purposes and not to harass or intimidate people. Respect for the law and for those who serve it should be shown. If you spend any time at a courthouse, you will notice that win or lose in any type of case, the attorneys get to walk freely from the courthouse. Make sure that this always remains true. Keeping your life and feelings of personal responsibility separate from your work is of utmost importance and very challenging on occasion. Your interests are always to be truthful to the court and that, even when tempted, you do not compromise your morals (and possibly your freedom and career) for a client, no matter what the circumstances.

As a lawyer you will be guided by personal conscience and also professional goals. Conflicts may arise between a lawyer's responsibilities to clients, to the legal system and to the lawyer's own interest in remaining an upright person while earning a satisfactory living. These issues can be resolved through professional and moral judgment. Every lawyer is responsible for observance of the Rules of Professional Conduct. A lawyer should also aid in observance by other lawyers. Neglect of these responsibilities comprises the independence of the profession and public interest, which it serves.

Lawyers should also seek improvement of the law. A lawyer can cultivate knowledge of the law in reform and work to strengthen legal education. You should acknowledge that sometimes a person couldn't afford adequate legal assistance at such times one should therefore devote professional time on their behalf. In many states there are even laws requiring a certain percentage of your legal work (or your firms' work) to be pro bono, or free of charge, for some charitable purpose. You are also required to have a certain amount of additional legal training each year to maintain your license to practice.

Don't Just Accept Lawyer Stereotypes

What do people think about lawyers? There are as many notions about lawyers as there are people. This section discusses a few of the stereotypes that you may encounter about lawyers. It might help in your decision making to think about some of these things. There are always stories in the media about unscrupulous lawyers who find loopholes and get a murderer out of jail. Some make you want to believe lawyers are the root of all-evil. But then there are stories about unselfish lawyers who give their time freely to a needy client and win. The bottom line is that you should make your own decision about what career is right for you, regardless of the stereotypes.

If lawyers are so bad then why do thousands of them each year represent clients for free? When someone is really in trouble why do they call their lawyer first? Why are so many lawyers honored for their contributions to society? If our legal system is so unjust why are developing democracies all over the world turning to us for help in defining their concepts of freedom and justice?

The most common stereotypes about lawyers are as follows: lawyers just get in the way, they actually create disputes that would not otherwise exist, lawyers are unscrupulous and dishonest, lawyers are greedy, they are interested in just making money and that there are too many of them.

Let's analyze some of these misconceptions. Do lawyers generate legal problems or interfere with their resolution. Let's start with the fundamental premises that generally, people do not seek a lawyer's advice because everything is going smoothly. People retain lawyers when they have a problem. We forget that lawyers represent people who come to them for help in solving problems that they could not work out for themselves. People go to lawyers because they believe that lawyers can get them things that they can't otherwise obtain. They feel that a lawyer will strongly defend their rights. And an attorney is usually the best person to defend them. Lawyers do not start out to delay a case; they represent clients who may ask them for certain things that may cause confusion.

Are lawyers unscrupulous? Are people in general unscrupulous? If you take a hundred people from any occupation you will find a certain number of them are unscrupulous. So you find the same thing in the legal profession.

Are lawyers greedy? Lawyers as a group make more money than

most people who lack high level educational training. But lawyers do not make as much money as most people think. Some lawyers receive average fees and some, whose reputation allows them, charge extremely high rates for their services. An average lawyer can expect a comfortable living but probably not as much as most doctors, top level business executives, professional athletes or successful computer software developers. Are lawyers greedy? Like in any profession there are always some.

Are there too many lawyers? The United States has more lawyers than any other country in the world. The Unites States also has more major corporations and businesses than any other country. This requires many more people with specialized knowledge of complicated legal issues as they relate to business such as in contracts, real estate, acquisitions and mergers, regulation or patent registration. The question of whether there are too many lawyers also might depend on your point of view. Lawyers already in practice may think there are too many lawyers. Yet there are many people, especially the poor that are not represented by lawyers. Most middle class people do not have a regular legal counsel. Despite the fact that most large cities have an over-supply of lawyers, many rural areas do not have enough.

Think about these stereotypes. This is what some people will define you as after you become a lawyer. You may even have to devote some time to defending your position on these concepts.

Balance in Your Life

Whatever career you chose you must achieve a balance in your life. The well-rounded happy person must learn to balance at least three components: family life, working and playing. The legal profession leaves little room for outside interests. Commitment to the law may produce an unbalanced life style, so make sure your career choice produces a well-rounded happy life. Seriously ask yourself "Would you have to give all of you efforts to your career in order to be in the legal profession?" If your answer is, "yes", then you may want to rethink you choice. The statistics of stress related situation, such as divorce, alcoholism, drug abuse, and burnout are disturbingly high for lawyers. This does not have to be your future. You can learn to balance your life as a lawyer if you pick the right type of law, environment, setting and are aware of your maximize capabilities.

Career Choice Process

Deciding if the legal profession is for you involves a career choice process through which you will make some major decisions about your life. There are two processes involved. The first step in the career choice process is self-analysis, finding your personal goals. The second process is the search, which includes your natural professional abilities to become a lawyer.

You should approach the career choice process in a rational way and take certain steps in sequence. If you are not sure about which way your professional life should go your must organize your thoughts. It is important that you have enough self-awareness and self-knowledge to be able to make a decision that will best satisfy your personal goals and professional abilities. In order to evaluate yourself you should consider your abilities, skills, needs, values and goals.

Not all lawyers need to master the same set of professional skills. This depends on what type of law you go into. The skills contributing to success in many legal careers are, problem solving, legal analysis and reasoning, legal research, factual investigation, communication, counseling, negotiation, litigation and alternative dispute resolution procedures, organization and management, and addressing ethical beliefs. Career theory suggests that people enjoy things they do well and that they will do well in the future in activities utilizing these skills. Look at these skills. Are they mostly what you are good at?

Deciding if the legal profession is for you involves a career choice process through which you will make some major decisions about your life. There are two processes involved. The first step in the career choice process is self-analysis, finding your personal goals. The second process is the search, which includes your natural professional abilities to become a lawyer.

Take a piece of paper and on one side write down what your personnel abilities, skills, needs values and goals are. Then on the other side of the paper write down what abilities, skills, needs, values and goals you think a lawyer will need. Do the sides match up? What do you need to work on to become a lawyer? Do you have most of the qualities? Would you be working on more of the skills then you think you should be? You want to achieve a balanced happy life, will becoming a lawyer achieve that for you? These are difficult questions and there are no easy answers. Here is a personality preference quiz that may help you analyze whether lawyering is for you:

1. Do you like to get emotionally involved with your wok?
2. Do you dislike or attempt to avoid conflict?
3. In resolving conflict, do you prefer deciding what's fair based on the circumstances of each situation?
4. Do you like to create or start projects and let others finish and or maintain them?
5. Do you dislike paying attention to details?
6. Do you prefer short-term projects?
7. Do you value efficiency?
8. Do you like to do things your own way, on your own schedule and in order of your own priorities?
9. Do you get more satisfaction being part of a team than being a solo act?
10. Do you want to change the world?

A "yes" answer to any of the above question should raise some reservations about entering the legal profession. Practicing law is attractive to people whose main enjoyment is dealing with important issues, like detail, value external rewards, status and security. If you thrive on interpersonal interaction, teamwork, or helping others you may find the emphasis on research, writing and legal analysis frustrating. There may be some appropriate options for you in the legal profession, but it does call for more thorough research.

Before Law School

Do some career planning before you apply to law school. Familiarize yourself with the actual law school experience. Are you looking at law school as a way to put off making a career decision? Are you seeking a law degree as a kind of Ph.D. in general studies that will qualify you for a professional position outside the legal profession? These may not be solid reasons for wanting to go to law school.

Familiarize yourself with the actual law school experience. Make a point of sitting in on a few law school classes. Pick up a law school textbook and study it. Talk to current law students and recent graduates. Ask them what value law school is having for them now, and what realistic opportunities await them.

Talk to many lawyers; those who enjoy practicing and those who do not. Talk to criminal prosecutors and defenders, civil litigates for the plaintiff and ask these practitioners to describe their typical week. Better yet, arrange to spend an entire day with one of them.

Values

Values are not only our personal morals but include our attitudes too. Some values lawyers should have are to provide competent representation, promoting justice, fairness, and morality, strive to improve the profession and professional self-development. There are many values a lawyer should have; these are just a few that should be incorporated into a lawyer's personality. Needing to represent people you do not like or trust is often necessary. Are you willing to do this?

What are the values a lawyer needs to possess? Can they be learned or are they genetically inherited? How does one acquire values? Are there certain critical legal values? Are some values more relevant to success in practice than others? Do lawyers as groups share a set of basic values? These are questions you must ask yourself and find the answer yourself. Do your answers fulfill your goals as a lawyer?

So What if You Don't Want to Be A Lawyer?

If you are one of those people who has read through this chapter and has come to the conclusion that you do not want to be a lawyer, you do not want to go through three years of school, you do not want to have the stress of handling cases themselves, and you do not want to be in thousands of dollars of debt, there is still opportunities for you in the legal field. You might want to consider a job as a paralegal. This type of shadow career is an excellent way to do the interesting, rewarding work of a lawyer, without some of the negative aspects of a lawyer's responsibilities. Obtaining certification differs in each state, but it often only takes a few months of full-time study. In some states, getting a job as a paralegal does not even require certification, although is highly recommended. As a paralegal you are not licensed to practice law, but help lawyers in their practice. You are often directly involved with the case, completing research and assisting attorneys with their needs, while often getting paid a very competitive salary. Like an attorney, paralegals specialize in various areas of law and their responsibilities vary depending on the size of the law firm they work for. As such, much of this book with still be very useful in making your way through a law firm and having a successful relationship with your firm.

The Good News About a Career in Law

A legal career prepares you for an almost unlimited array of opportunities. Knowledge of the law is useful in most aspects of life and necessary in many. In a complex society contact with the law becomes increasingly more important. If you decide to go into law your law degree uses are limited only by your own imagination and your awareness of the opportunities. You will be choosing a career that will allow you to help the world while giving you a balanced happy life.

Law is not a career but many careers. For those willing to enter this environment law offers and an exciting challenge. There are many different ways to practice law and not all require the same type of person. You can find the right position in law for you. The decision to pursue a career in law involves finding a place within this system where individual skills, values and goals can thrive in a well-balanced manner.

Conclusion

After reading this chapter you now are more aware of why you want to be a lawyer. You considered the many issues of the law profession before making a decision. A simple questionnaire enabled you to find out what you can expect from a law career and how to achieve your goals. You examined your strengths and weaknesses in order to find the right place in the law profession for you and to achieve a balanced successful life.

This chapter also delved into the many stereotypes of lawyers and how this may effect your decision on becoming one yourself. It discussed the values and morals you will have to accept and abide by as a lawyer. It also helped you through the career choice process by explaining the two processes involved. Through self-analysis and searching you were able to make a better career choice to satisfy your personal goals.

"For anyone contemplating becoming a Lawyer..."

So You Want To Be A
Lawyer?

Official
Know-it-All
Guide

Marianne Pilgrim Calabrese
Susanne Mary Calabrese

Chapter Two

Law School and the Bar Exam

As you master your destiny, you need to identify what you want from your career and create a plan to achieve your goals. This chapter has shown you ways to know what you want from a career and how to get it. One secret to success in creating your career plan is through change. Don't be afraid of change and believe in yourself.

The competition to get into law school is intense and applicants to most law schools greatly exceed the number that can be admitted. Depending on the law school, thousands, even tens of thousands of applicants can apply for only a few hundred openings. Since the competition is so great there are some things you should know in order to better your chances of getting into law school. Factors such as college grades, class rank, letters of recommendation, essays, personnel interviews, extracurricular activities, work experience, career goals, geographic background, quality of an undergraduate institution including the extent to which grade inflation has occurred, the difficulty of your major field, LSAT, what law school you apply to and any other graduate level study you may have all affect your application to law school.

In actuality, your first assignment should be to view admission into law school as your first big case. You are going to be arguing before a court, (a.k.a. the admissions committee) Your evidence is your merits for acceptance into their program (a.k.a. the credentials on your application to law school). Most law schools will make their decision on the basis of a brief, (a.k.a. your application). Your goal is to argue persuasively why you should be admitted to their law school by marketing yourself effectively.

Law schools require applicants to use the Law School Data

Assembly Service (LSDAS) to prepare and provide a report for each school to which you want to apply. The report includes your academic undergraduate record, copies of official transcripts, LSAT scores, writing samples and copies of letters of recommendations. LSDAS will then compile a report that is sent to all the law schools to which you apply.

There is little room for mistakes, such as a bad semester, a wrong choice of majors or a year or two of too much partying. Some law school admission committees may overlook a few things and not take into consideration one bad semester, but every time you falter you lessen your chances of eventually getting into law school. It is hard to accept that something you did years ago will seriously damage your law school application, but those who are serious about law school can overcome the challenges. Law is a tough field and it starts before law school. If you do have blemishes on your academic record, you must take extra care on your application to highlight your strong points.

How Law Schools Choose Students

There is no rhyme or reason on how law schools choose their students. Every school keys in on different factors. Some schools admit students 'by the number,' usually a combination of undergraduate grade point average (GPA) and the Law School Admission Test (LSAT) scores. Other schools look at a number of factors such as extracurricular activities, work experience, geographic location, difficulty of major and other considerations that don't show up in your GPA. Most schools do not just look at GPA scores. It would be wise to try to find out what factors the schools you are apply to are most interested in. Most law schools look for the applicant's ability to demonstrate an aptitude for the study of law.

You should apply to several law schools to increase your chances of being accepted. You may have all the academic qualities but wind up being rejected or waitlisted because there is already somebody like you in the class. In recent years admissions to law school has become more and more difficult. It can be a very frustrating process.

Law School Admission Test (LSAT)

The Law School Admission Test (LSAT) is a standardized test taken by all prospective law students. All law schools approved by the ABA, except those in Puerto Rico require applicants to take the LSAT.

It consists of five multiple-choice sections, each thirty five minutes in length and one thirty minute writing section. The multiple-choice sections are divided into two Logical Reasoning sections (which contains various short-answer questions), one Logic Games section (which contains four logic games with five to seven short answer questions pertaining to each), one Reading Comprehension section (which contains four short passages with five to seven short answer questions pertaining to each) and one Experimental section that does not count towards your score and can be any of the above. The thirty minute writing section also does not count toward your score, but is sent to all the law schools you apply to as a sample of your writing ability.

The test is designed to predict law school success by testing such skills as analyzing problems, and critical reading. You should definitely prepare thoroughly for the LSAT. Taking a course or studying on your own are both effective ways to prepare for the test. Some schools state there is a high correlation between LSAT scores and the first year law student's grades. If you do well on the LSAT great, if you don't do well or if you feel the LSAT is not an accurate reflection of your ability to study law, you should indicate that on your application, as many schools leave space to explain such factors. You may also want to consider taking them over, but be warned most law schools average your LSAT scores together.

Undergraduate Major

There is no recommended "prelaw" major. You should develop abilities in writing, speaking, reading, researching, analyzing, and thinking logically. These are skills needed to succeed in law school and in the profession. Law students have majored in almost every subject, political science, business, history, the technical sciences, education, music and the arts, psychology, liberal arts and even drama to name a few. There are innumerable theories about which majors are best, but the best choice is the one you made yourself. If you have an undergraduate degrees in basic liberal arts subjects that stress analytical thinking and core knowledge it will give you a good foundation for study in various types of law. Your undergraduate major may help you decide what type of law you will go into. For example, if you major in accounting and love it, you may want to go into tax law. If you majored in psychology you will now have an understanding of the way people think, which can be very useful in dealing with judges, juries, witnesses and clients. If you major in theater you have learned to project your voice and developed acting abilities which will come in handy when litigating a case.

Some larger colleges and universities with their own law schools offer pre-law undergraduate programs that take you all the way through an undergraduate program and into a Juris Doctor (JD degree), law program at the graduate level. Such programs generally concentrate on course work in the liberal arts and may or may not confer a separate bachelor's degree after four years of study.

What is the Best Law School for Me?

The American Bar Association approved more than 180-law schools in the United States. There are other law schools that are not approved. What is the difference? How do you know which school to apply to and which is the best for you. First try to apply to schools you have a chance of getting into and that are approved. Schools that are approved by ABA enable you to practice law in any state. If the law school is only approved in the state it is located then that is the only state you can practice law in.

How do you know which school to apply to and which is the best for you? Essentially you have to judge which school would be the best by the things that are the most important to you. You obviously want to get into the best law school you can. But your choice of law school should also depend on which factors are most important to you. Some factors that you should think about are; the type of law you want to practice, geographical area where you would like to live, faculty involvement you would prefer, library facilities, campus size, notoriety, alumni support, special programs and cost.

When you are looking at prospective schools, you must ask yourself many important questions about the way you will live your life for the next three years. Who is on the faculty? What is the ratio of students to faculty? How many volumes are in the library? Does it have an up to date filing system? How many legally trained staff members are there? Are there sufficient classrooms and seminar rooms? Is there a courtroom? Is there a career library, counseling, career information panels and training in job search skills. What are the tuition fees? What financial aid is available? Your choice of law school should depend on which factors are most important to you and which school provides them. So before you send that application, don't make the number one mistake made by applicants and simply look at the rankings. Although going to a top ranked law school will give you more job opportunities in the future, not every top school is right for every person. Do yourself a big favor and find out if the school has most of the things that you personally need to have a wonderful three years.

How to Get Into Law School

There are three basic rules you need to abide by in order to better your chances of getting into law school.
They are:

1. Keep your academic record in high order, take extra care on your application to highlight your strong points
2. Apply to a minimum of nine law schools Make sure at least three are ones you feel you will be accepted to, even if they may not be your first three choices. Although the application fees are costly, in the end the sum will be well worth it to ensure the right placement for you.
3. Prepare for the LSAT. Take a course or study with a group but prepare. Do whatever you must do to get the highest grade on the LSAT. If you don't do well and you feel it was not an accurate reflection of your ability then indicate that on your application.

Financing your Legal Education

Going to law school is an expensive endeavor. Even after paying tuition (which even at the least expensive school would cost several thousands), you will need to pay for books, room and board, and miscellaneous fees. If you are like the majority of applicants you will be taking out loans for law school. According to the Law School Admissions Council, currently, the average debt for law school graduates who borrowed both federal and privately guaranteed student loans is about $80,000. Law school graduate debt of $80,000 amounts to almost $1,000 a month on a ten-year repayment plan. Unless you are one of the lucky few that are able to afford the tuition, how much and how you pay for law school is an incredibly important factor to consider. Loans put enormous pressure on you to obtain a high paying position when you graduate, thus narrowing your career choices. If you can find a way to pay for law school without having to work or assume loans do it.

If you cannot or will not assume such a large amount of debt and you still want to be a lawyer, there are other ways to attend school. Schools that are subsidized by the state are also an excellent bargain and can save you tens of thousands of dollars. Research closely law schools in your state. You might even consider taking time off before law school in order to set up residency in a neighboring state; it might be well worth your time. You may also want to work for a time before law school in order to save money. Another possibility is attending law school part-time. Many of the country's top law schools offer night programs where students are able to take fewer credits (for less cost), enabling them to still work during the day. A student in the night program graduates in four years, (instead of three in a day program) but is usually conferred the same diploma as day students. Working during the day and going to school at night can be exhausting, but will save you thousands of dollars. And if you feel you cannot attend school at night anymore, transferring to the day program is usually very easy.

A large percentage of entering law students wish to practice public interest law, law dealing with the interests of people. The clients themselves often define the specialty by their needs. Unfortunately, only a few actually pursue this field after graduation because of financial concerns and high debt from student loans. Luckily, more and more law schools are adapting programs of loan forgiveness for those students who pursue a career in public interest, giving more incentive to enter the field.
Try to take care of your finances before enrolling and by all means think realistically about how they will affect you after graduation. Don't put yourself into so much debt that you will be paying off loans longer than you want to or that you will have to take a law position you hate just for the money.

Accepted to Law School

When you do get accepted into law school many question will go through your mind. You might even question if you really want to go. This is natural; it is a major decision and it has major consequences. Going to law school can be a mind-expanding experience and may be the most exciting time of your life. If you have already thought very hard before you started your journey into the application process, there is no need to second-guess yourself now that you've been accepted to law school. But if for some reason, you have forgotten why it is that you want to be a lawyer in the first place. Think about your goals and desires for success and a balanced life. Being accepted into law school means you, most likely, have what it takes to graduate and become a lawyer.

The American Bar Association wants law students to complete at least eighty four semester hours. This is usually a three or four year program. First year courses are usually core courses: Lawyering skills, torts, contracts, and property. Other law courses can be criminal law, constitutional law, civil law procedure, and introduction to the legal system. In the remaining time, you may elect specialized courses in fields such as labor, tax, environmental, bankruptcy, criminal or corporate law. Each school has some program to teach legal research, writing and oral advocacy skills during the first year. The curriculum varies from school to school after the first year.

You may acquire practical experience by participating in school sponsored legal clinic activities. Moot court competitions, in which students conduct appellate arguments, mock trial competitions which are practice trials under the supervision of experienced lawyers and judges, or school's various law journals which highlight research and writing on legal issues are all great ways to gain experience. A number of law schools also have clinical programs in which students gain legal experience through practice trials and projects under the supervision of practicing lawyers and law school faculty. Law school clinical programs might include work in legal aid clinics in anything from domestic violence to child advocacy or on the staff of legislative committees. Part time or summer clerkships in law firms, government agencies and corporate legal departments also provide valuable experience. Such training can lead directly to a job after graduation and can help you decide what kind of practice best suits you.

Law school, at the very least can be described as complex and challenging. Think very hard before you start your journey into law school. Some feel that lawyers become abusive when law professors utilizing the

Socratic Method, verbally batter them, thereby turning out "mean spirited attorneys who browbeat their opponents and mistreat clients" Before law school some feel lawyers were human beings with compassion, intelligence, love and mirth. After law school most of those quantities will be replaced and now the lawyer has ambition, ego, compulsive inclination and a competitive nature. Although this stereotype is rather exaggerated, there is some truth to the fact that law school will change the way you see the world and thus will change the way you react to it. You might want to keep this in mind before you start law school. Law school, like most higher education, changes anyone who goes through it. It is much more than learning the law, it is an experience in learning how to solve problems. The core of it is the interaction between students and faculty.

It changes anyone who goes through it. It will transform your habits and the way you think. It is much more than learning the law, it its an experience in learning how to solve problems. The core of it is the interaction between students and faculty.

The Socratic Teaching Method

Many of the law professors use the Socratic Method when teaching law students. Professors who rely on the Socratic Method today use participatory learning and discussions with a few students on whom they call randomly to explore very difficult legal concepts and principles. Most likely you will have about a hundred students in your law classes and the best way the law professors found to provide active learning in large classes is calling on students without giving them prior notice. The professor will call on one student to discuss in detail a case they were assigned. The professor will then rapid-fire questions based on the law, legal reasoning and its application to a particular case. Other students should be pondering the legal questions posed while their classmate answers them. You will not know before classes whether you will be called on to discuss difficult issues or to respond to answers provide by another student. Therefore you must always be prepared and pay close attention to the discussions. The responsibility will be on you to think about the questions silently and participate actively on your own. The element of surprise provides a powerful incentive for you to meet that responsibility.

Many students view the Socratic Method with enormous trepidation.

You may worry about speaking in front of a large group that includes your professor. Speaking in public, whether in the courtroom, before a group of clients or opposing counsel, or in a meeting of lawmakers wording to draft a statute, is part of every lawyer's job. So developing the ability to present ideas forcefully and effectively is integral part of becoming a lawyer. You may be very anxious about making mistakes when you are called on. Making mistakes in class is inevitable and ultimately helpful as you work toward solutions to difficult legal problems.

Professors are more likely to focus on questions that lack clear answers and problems that defy simple solutions. This can cause you to become frustrated by the uncertainty and superficial indeterminacy. Your feelings of unease and discomfort may be heightened during the first year when the Socratic method is the dominant teaching style because you are confronting a new vocabulary, and an unfamiliar logical analysis. Your law professor use the Socratic method to provide you greater confidence about talking to large groups, allows you to develop the ability to argue forcefully and persuasively and teachers you to think critically.

The goal is to learn how to analyze legal problems to reason by analogy, to think critically about one's own arguments and thoughts put forth by others, and to understand the effect of the law on those subject to it. You will find you have to articulate, develop and defend positions that may at first be imperfectly defined intuitions in law school. You may remember Professor Kingsfield from the movie the Paper Chase and the terror his students felt every time they entered his contract class. Law school classes are indeed somewhat like that.

In order to be a lawyer you have to first and foremost be a problem solver, and the primary task of law school is to equip you with the tools you need to solve problems. The law will change over the course of your career and the problems you confront will vary tremendously. Law professor cannot provide you with the answers but they can provide you help developing reasoning skills that you can apply, regardless of the legal question.

You will find your law school experience is what you make it. Knowledge of the law will become most important in your life. So take advantage of all your school has to offer such as faculty office hours, career center help sessions, volunteer legal clinics and other extracurricular activities that will make your experience rewarding and fulfilling. Make sure you go to any activities your professors invite you to and learn to socialize with them. This will help you stand out in the crowd. Remember your professor can be a wealth of possibilities when seeking a position or letter of recommendation.

If You Don't Get Into Law School

If, for some reason, you do not get into law school, it is not because you are not bright enough, or because you don't have what it takes, sometimes life just has other things planned for you. There is always next year to apply, and never fear, this section is dedicated to other options.

Refine your application. By now you probably have a good idea of what areas of your application was the weakest. Did you not have enough work experience or community service? Did you not have a clear idea of why you wanted to go to law school? Take this opportunity to volunteer for some activities in your community, get involved with service or activism, and try out another job opportunity. Not only will this make your application stronger for next year, but also you may find something else you really love to do. You may want to take the LSAT again. Make sure you do your homework and apply to schools you have a chance of getting into. Don't apply to just reach schools hoping that luck will get you into one of them. Apply to schools that have accepted applicants with your credentials, even if they are not your top choices.

In the mean time there are many opportunities in the legal profession for you if you do not go to law school. It is possible to work in a law office or perform law related work in many jobs where bar membership is not a prerequisite. There are shadow professions, like paralegal, legal assistants, case assistants, legal clerks and legal secretaries that also work in the legal field. Paralegal assist attorneys with their cases and in some states are even allowed to perform routine legal services.

Professional positions can include top level managers, the law firm administrator or office manager, director of personnel, recruiting director, law librarian, information technology director, marketing director, salary and benefits administrator, educational director and accountant. Some firms hire specialist to work directly with the legal service delivery team such as investigators, researcher analysts and even experts, for example engineers. Some firms create ancillary business ventures such as consulting firms. There are growing opportunities for business, computer science, human resources, marketing and accounting majors in law as well as for librarians, economists, statisticians and other specialists within the law firm.

It is not the end of the world if you did not get into law school this year. Maybe taking a year to fine tune your application or apply to better potential schools and working in the law field will open up a whole new world for you. Remember one does not need to go to law school to find work in the legal profession. Law related professionals, paralegal, and clerical employees can all work within the legal profession.

The Bar Exam

Once you graduate law school you have to pass the bar exam in order to practice law. The requirements and examinations vary from state to state. Forty eight states, the District of Columbia, Guam the Northern Mariana Islands, Puerto Rico and the Virgin Islands require the 6 hour Multistate Bar Examination (MBE) as part of the overall bar examination; the MBE is not required in Louisiana and Washington. The MBE covers issues of broad interest, and sometimes a locally prepared State bar examination is given in addition to the MBE. The three-hour Multistate Essay Examination (MEE) is also used as part of the bar examination in several states. States vary in their use of MBE and MEE scores.

Many states have begun to require Multistate Performance Testing (MPT) to test the practical skills of beginning lawyers. This Program has been well received and many more states are expected to require performance testing in the future. Requirements vary by state, although the test usually is taken at the same time as the bar exam and is a one-time requirement. Some states will let you take it during law school, usually after completing a course on legal ethics.

In 2001, law students in 52 jurisdictions were required to pass the Multistate Professional Responsibility Examination (MPRE) which tests their knowledge of the ABA Codes of Professional Responsibility and Judicial Conduct. In some states the MPRE may also be taken during law school, usually after completing a course on legal ethics.

You will be subjected to strict procedures, forms and a character and fitness investigation in order to take the bar exam. In most jurisdictions this includes providing a set of fingerprints to the Board of Bar Examiners and revealing confidential medical information about some psychological treatment, diagnoses or hospitalizations. If you do not pass this investigation you will not be allowed to take the exam or you will be denied admission to the state bar even if you achieved a score sufficient to pass the examination. If you have been convicted of a crime or engaged in immoral activities,, you may have difficulty being certified to take the exam. Bar review courses are given in most states and it is highly recommended that you take one.

Some may feel the bar exam is supported by practicing lawyers to reduce competition and discourage mobility and not just to ensure a strong legal knowledge for attorneys. This may or may not be true. Either way you still have to pass the bar exam in your state in order to practice law.

Law school graduates receive the degree of Juris Doctor (J.D.) as the first professional degree. Advanced law degrees may be desirable for those planning to specialize, do research or teach. You can pursue a joint degree program, which usually require an additional semester or year of study. Joint degree programs are offered in a number of areas, including law, international relations and business administration or public administration.

After graduation, you most likely will have to continue your legal education. Forty states and jurisdictions mandate continuing legal education. Many law schools and state and local bar associations provide continuing education courses that help lawyers stay updated within their field. Some states allow credits to be obtained through participation in seminars on the Internet.

Tips to Find Happiness

If possible resist the pressure to enter private practice from law school. If you entered law to have a positive impact on either individuals or on society, find a position that satisfies that desire. Although the high salaries and security of private business are attractive be aware that these same influences can also become traps. Unhappy lawyers agree that it is very difficult, both emotionally and practically to make a change that has the appearance of stepping down the ladder of success.

Free Information

The American Bar Association publishes, "A Review of Legal Education in the United States", which gives information on the law schools approved by the ABA, state requirements for admission to legal practice, a directory of state bar examination administrators and other information on legal education. Single copies are free from the ABA. You can search their website at www.abanet.org, or you may also get information from:

Member Services

American Bar Association

750 North Lake Shore Drive

Chicago, IL 60611-3314

Information on the LSAT, the Law School Data Assemble Service, applying to law school, and financial aid for law students may be obtained from, the Law School Admission's Council website at www.lsac.org or by writing to:

Law School Admission Services

P.O. Box 40

Newtown, PA 18940

Specific requirements for admission to the bar in a state or other jurisdiction may be obtained at the state capital, from the clerk of the Supreme Court, or the administrator of the State Board of Bar Examiners. Most of this information is easily accessibly on the internet.

Conclusion

This chapter helped you to better your chances of getting into law school. It gave you clear-cut ideas about your academic records, LSAT scores, and what law schools to apply to get into a law school that is best for you.

It gave you insights into how law school's choose students and why and what law school would be best for you. This chapter enabled you to realize what things are most important to you when applying to law school. Factors such as type of law, environment, faculty, library facilities, notary, special programs finance and your chances of getting in were discussed to help you make a decision about which law school to apply to. You were presented with three hints on how to get into a law school.

Chapter 2 also enlightened you on how and what to do when you are accepted into law school and also what to do if you are not. The Bar examination, Multistate Bar Examination, Multistate Essay Examination, Multistate Professional Responsibility Examination and the Multistate Performance Testing are discussed fully so you know what is expected after graduation from law school.

"For anyone contemplating becoming a Lawyer..."

So You Want To Be A
Lawyer?

Official
Know-It-All
Guide

Marianne Pilgrim Calabrese
Susanne Mary Calabrese

Chapter Three

Law Practice Environment

Basic History of the Law

One type or another law practice has been around almost as long as mankind itself. The first legal system recorded was the Code of Hammurabi, named after the Mesopotamian ruler who adopted it about 1900BC. The code was a series of laws that defined crimes and what the punishment would be. It put society's rules in writing thus eliminating any confusion. Until then, laws were made by a ruler who could change them at will. Hammurabi's Code made sure that Mesopotamia was run according to the rule of law, a concept that became one of the most cherished principles of modern, free societies.

Law also has roots in ancient Greek and Roman times. At one time the laws were basic, and thus clearly understood by all people, effectively generating no need for lawyers. But as society became more complex so did the laws. A group of Roman aristocrats studied and developed the law. They became known as special legal advisors or juris consults. Eventually the Romans developed a more formal system with orators studying the law and presenting cases. Procurators wrote up documents and litigation began. Law schools were created with professors to teach citizens about the law. The Roman legal system spread and as a result, much of the legal profession throughout Europe has its foundation from the Romans.

After the Norman Conquest, English royal courts developed what is known as, "Common Law". Common law was mostly unwritten and was based on custom and precedent. Later, "Equity" came into practice, which was based on the dictates of conscience filling in the gaps in justice left by the common law. And later still, in the 18th century, the theory of "Natural Law" based on the natural rights of humans was stressed.

Lawyers in Literature

Shakespeare's most famous lawyer line, "The first thing we should do, let's kill all the lawyers," is not the condemnation we have come to think of it as. In fact, within the context of the play Henry VI, in Part II, (Act IV), Scene 2, it is actually an endorsement of the legal profession. The accolade is spoken by Dick the Butcher, a follower of anarchist Jack Cade, whom Shakespeare depicts as "the head of an army of rabble and a demagogue pandering to the ignorant," who sought to overthrow the government. He wanted to replace a system of laws with a dictatorship based on personal power. To Shakespeare, the rebels were a threat to order and justice, while lawyers stood in the path of anarchy. The quote actually reveals that Shakespeare was paying homage to the profession as guardians of society.

However, long before our Founding Fathers formed our legal system, Sir Thomas Moore's Uttiopia circa 1516, declared that in a utopian society, the citizens, "They have no lawyers among them for they consider them as a sort of people whose profession is to disguise matters." There has always been a love hate relationship between lawyers and society.

Lawyers in the United States

The English exported their legal system to the American Colonies. In the later years, lawyers were praised as the drafters of the Declaration of Independence and the Constitution, but they were excluded from some to the earliest American colonies. After the Revolution, lawyers became the new aristocracy after longstanding ties to the British monarchy were broken. Because of this, anti-lawyer sentiment festered from the colonial period and lawyers were in disfavor during most of the nineteenth century.

In those times any one who wanted to become a lawyer could do so by reading law books until he was ready to take an oral examination from a qualified member of the bar. The image of Abraham Lincoln studying his law books by firelight in rural Illinois and eventually parlaying his skills into a political career represents the spirit of that era of law. Other lawyers of Lincoln's period served apprenticeships to practicing lawyers, but only a small percentage were formally educated in law schools.

The first American law school, Harvard Law School opened in the United States in 1817. The standardization of the bar examination was established, the adoption of ethical codes and the evolution of strong self-regulating bar associations evolved. These changes helped to overcome contemporary negative reaction to the legal profession.

Although there is still a love hate relationship with the legal profession today, history has shown the legal profession has always maintained an important position in America society. We are a nation founded on legal principles and we frequently use lawyers to help strike the balance of power between order and liberty and between individual and state or Federal government. Lawyers have been faithful civil servants, holding positions in all branches of government: the executive legislative and judicial branches of government at the federal, state, and local level. Lawyers have been involved in every aspect of this country's growth from colonial times to present and will continue to do so.

Different Law Environments

All the different types of lawyers and their roles can work in private practice, corporations, government, non-profit, education, group and prepaid legal services and entrepreneurs. You will do most of your work in offices, law libraries, or on the computer and courtrooms. Sometimes you will meet clients in their homes or places of business and when necessary in hospitals or prisons. You have to pick the environment that will work best for you. The type of law you practice will determine where the most openings are.

Private Practice

The largest numbers of lawyers are employed in private practice where they concentrate on criminal or civil law. Instead of selling their time to one employer, private practitioners work for different clients. The private practitioners are entrepreneurs that must make enough money to run their own business. If you go into private practice you must accept the fact that law is a business and you must make a profit in order to stay in business.

There is the solo group of private practitioners; these lawyers practice alone with a legal staff. Some solo practitioners employ ten or more personnel such as paralegals, secretaries, investigators and others. If you are a good solo practitioner and businessperson you can make a good profit in this type of situation. Solo practitioners do however, statistically show the lowest per capita income of any group of attorneys.

There are benefits such as the freedom of being your own boss and making all the decisions. You will not have to answer to any other partners. You can open your business where you want. However it is difficult to be a self-employed lawyer mostly because of the significant cost of starting a new business and partly because many lawyers especially recent graduates lack the skills and experience necessary to practice competently alone. Solo practitioners have usually worked in larger firms and can network with other lawyers when the need arises.

There are many firms that are opened between family members or with groups of law school friends after a few years of private practice in a large firm. Opening your own firm is just like opening your own business – you must have your own clients in order to pay the rent and costs of doing business. If you have made a name for yourself, or if you can partner with colleagues who have well-paying clients, this is often a gamble that may pay-off very well. One large corporate client is enough to support a small firm. Starting your own firm is also a quick way to earn the title of partner, with which you can transfer laterally to other firms. The downside is that like any small business, small law firms often have a hard time paying their bills, especially since clients of lawyers are inherently more difficult to collect on-time payments from. The risk of not making a profit, the constant need to look for new clients once cases finish, and the difficulties in administrating a law firm can make this venture difficult.

Entrepreneurs go into business for themselves. They manage and market their business skills in many law areas such as real estate, commercial development, financial joint ventures, consultants and writing. If you decide to become an entrepreneur you will have to be experienced in many areas of the law with a good established networking system. You are essentially opening up your own business and you are the sole owner and worker. Often the most successful entrepreneurs have special knowledge of the law or an area of expertise that they may hire themselves out as an independent contractor. If you are considering law as a second career, you previous experience coupled with a law degree might prove very useful in this type of job.

Large, Medium and Small Law Firms

The highest paid group of private lawyers practice in large law firms. A large law firm is usually considered to have a hundred lawyers or more. They tend to be located in large cities. They usually have long-standing prestigious reputations and clients to match. These firms generally grew to such a large size to accommodate all the needs of large corporate clients' such as banks, insurance companies, industrial as well as large private estates and organizations.

Large firms tend to have the highest salaries for recent law school graduates, and for this reason competition for these positions is intense. If you do get a position in one of these firms your workload will be demanding and you will have a one in ten chance of becoming a partner. Sometimes working in a smaller branch office of a large firm offers an alternative for you to become part of the larger organization while working in an office that has the atmosphere of a smaller law firm.

A branch office is a location in a different city than the headquarters of the large firm. Most big firms have national clients and thus, have several locations across the country. Some of these offices are large, however, many of them are much smaller than others, but still have a strong connection with the other larger offices. You will be expected to work long hours including holidays. The firm will establish a goal, usually high number of billable hours that you will have to work toward each year.

Billable hours are the time that can be billed for legal service to the client. Even in small firms there may be pressure to produce billable hours. Many associates in firms work long hours for years only to be told that they will not be offered a more lucrative partnership position. Billing hours are incredibly important to the firm because they charge clients based on an hourly rate. The more time you bill a client, the more money the firm makes.

There are firms that lie in the middle of very large firms and small firms. These are firms for one reason or another that have not grown as large as their competitors or to branch out into other cities. It includes law firms that are the largest in small cities but have not opened many branches in other locations. They may be as small as fifteen or twenty lawyers or as large as fifty or hundred depending on the size of the legal needs in the city they are located. When the law firm gets somewhere between ten and twenty-five lawyers it begins to departmentalize. They subdivide along practice areas thus transforming individual practices into group practices. Medium size firms may be the remnants of other law firms that have split up in the past. Law firms are constantly changing. Small firms grow into medium and then large firms, and large firms break up into smaller ones. As a lawyer you are likely to work in several different law firms over the course of your career and even if you decide to stay in one firm it is likely you will experience a series of changes in that one firm.

The largest part of private practice is made up of small law firms. The legal profession is mostly small firm work. They are less likely to depend on large institutional clients for business. Most of these are general practices and rely on many different types of clients. There is a trend of the smaller law firms becoming more specialized. Your chances are about one in three of working for one of these types of firms during your career.

Most lawyers earn a relatively good income, however lawyers in smaller firms and in teaching positions often do not earn more than individuals with only an undergraduate education. High income is in no way guaranteed even if you are in private practice. It will depend on the ability of the firm to attract and keep clients and your ability to service them.

Corporations

If you become an in- house lawyer you may practice a variety of legal work. You will have one employer, the corporation. The largest numbers of corporate lawyers work as in- house counsels who practice law inside the corporation in a law department. Law departments can range from one or two attorneys to several hundred. The role of the department can rage from providing advice to top management, to handling legislative work, to managing outside counsel, to providing full service in house legal support. In-house law departments tend to be more hierarchical than in a small law firm. Usually one general counsel, several associate general counsels and many assistant general counsels work in a department.

Some in- house lawyers are not in any specific legal department because they supply a unique skill. They may provide legal advice to management and perform other managerial or administrative work. The companies that hire these types of lawyers are usually small. The benefit of this type of positions is that you may have an opportunity to grow with the company and eventually become the head of a growing law department.

There is also the advantage of becoming exposed to many types of law including immigration, real estate, tax and patent law. Every corporation has legal needs. The main idea of a legal department within the corporation is to pay in-house lawyers rather than expensive lawyers from an independent firm in order to lower their legal fees. Most of the time, in-house lawyers save the corporation a lot of money in legal costs. An attorney in a small corporation may have responsibilities other then the legal affairs. Some corporations hire new lawyers to handle legal problems and assume management duties too. A practice in a corporation provides a diversity of experiences for lawyers but it may prove to be an incredibly stressful position as well.

If you become an in- house corporate lawyer you will probably have a better salary then in a law firm. Fringe benefits like mobility, insurance, employee saving plans and. retirement also tend to be better in corporations because even small businesses tend to employ more people then large law firms. Corporations may offer stock options or other financial incentives as well, that a law firm would not.

When you compare large and small corporate law departments there are some significant differences. In a large corporation the company operations may be so diverse that you may have the feeling that you are working for a number of clients. You usually specialize as a lawyer in a large corporation and you may have a practice that is much closer to that of a lawyer in a large law firm than a lawyer in a small firm. The practice in a small corporate law department may be more like that in a small firm where you will be expected to do a myriad of different tasks for one client. The benefit is that you will have the opportunity to gain valuable experience and grow with the company. Often where there are fewer people to perform the many tasks necessary in a case, an inexperienced lawyer will be given more meaningful responsibility at a smaller firm.

The corporate law department may offer some unusual opportunities for a junior attorney. Generally, corporations don't even look at new law graduates because they don't have the resources to train new lawyers. Most companies won't look at an applicant who doesn't have at least 3 years experience. You may likely be more closely involved in the running of the business, in such things as determining policy and becoming involved in management. In a big company you may have a feeling of being isolated from the action, or not understanding how one's work actually fits into the organization. This can be frustrating to someone who needs to see the results of her or his work.

The large size corporate giants can offer some fringe benefits. If you are unhappy in one department there is a good possibility you can transfer to another. If you want to travel there are likely opportunities to transfer to a department more well suited to your needs. For example, some corporations may even enable you to enter the field of international law. In many corporations, experienced lawyers fill the overseas positions while the new lawyers may find themselves doing the international practice in law libraries in domestic law offices.

Corporate law departments are growing rapidly and they are using the law school graduate to meet their employment needs. It is clear that practice in a corporation is a viable career path in the legal profession today.

Government

Government positions give lawyers two important assets, expertise in a particular field of law and contacts that may lead to clients in private practices. The government agencies where you can work are federal, military, state, judicial, city, and quasi-governmental. Government position can give you more security and better working hours than private practice. But the financial rewards are usually a lot less.

If you want to work for the federal government, it is the largest government service. The positions tend to be in Washington D.C. The United Stated Law Department is the largest law firm in the world; it has one client, the United States. Most of the work is litigation within the many divisions. The Internal Revenue Service also employs a large number of lawyers with special training in taxes and accounting. Also there is the United States District Court a branch of the United States Attorney office.

The military also hires civilian and military lawyers. Primarily lawyers are in the military Judge Advocate General's Corp or JAG. These officers are usually recruited straight from law school or sometimes sent to law school in return for a commitment to work at JAG. If you work in this department you can serve on military agencies around the world, representing service men and women in cases form court martial to disputes involving civilian issues. You can also be a civil lawyer in areas such government contracts.

State governments have many departments like the federal government. All states have an attorney general office, tax division, education department and other components. If you work for a state government the issues will be more localized and you may have opportunities for positions in administration, as hearing officers and research analysis.

In the judicial branch of government, lawyers can serve as judges, law clerks and judicial administrators. Most judges are experienced and respected lawyers. Law clerking will give you the opportunity to learn the judicial system by working for a judge, conducting research, and completing many other forms of assistance. These positions provide you with excellent credentials to further your career and are highly coveted.

Local government lawyers usually function like in house lawyers, of course this depends on the size of the local government. Usually separate departments represent the city or county in civil matters and prosecute violations of the law in stare or local courts. Also legal positions with many local boards and authorities are available.

The quasi-governmental work includes agencies that constitute joint ventures between the public and the private sector. If you like politics and want to eventually run for office a government law position may be for you.

Nonprofit Law

The Legal Services Corporation provides legal services to Americans who cannot otherwise afford representation. These law positions are usually government-funded positions. Other forms of nonprofit law are specific political action, law reform, and public interest groups. America has become a nation of interest groups, and nonprofits have become more and more important. These include private organizations, professional associations, citizen watchdog groups, campaign fund raising committees, religious groups and benevolent organizations.

Education

Lawyers are employed in all levels of education. As a lawyer you can work as a college professor high school teacher, primary educator, administrative agent or school district counselor. You can also present workshops, speak for education programs and host information seminars. It is also possible to supplement your position in private practice with a teaching position. Not only does this improve your resume and vastly increase your academic resources, it can greatly improve your networking with other prominent attorneys that are often on the faculty.

Group and Prepaid Legal Services

Group legal services can be compared to medical HMO while prepaid legal services resemble medical insurance. They were developed to provide affordable legal services to the middle class. Group legal services are often provided through some trade or professional association such as a union. If you work as a lawyer in this type of atmosphere you most likely will work for an independent private practitioner and the form of pay will vary. Under a prepaid plan, clients would be reimbursed for legal expenses and selects the lawyers of their choice. These types of plans have not been widely used by the general public.

How to Find an Environment That Will Satisfy Your Needs

The following questions will help you target the type of legal work that most appeals to you. Before you answer each questions, make sure you are responding to your own feelings and not to what you believe would most impress others or meet the expectations of your family, friends, or colleagues. When you have answered all the questions, and have a clearer vision of your preferences, incorporate the answers into a description of your ideal legal position. Then begin to research the job market to locate jobs that fit that description.

What Are Your Work Values?

1. To help people?
2. To help businesses?
3. To meet intellectual challenges?
4. To study thoroughly points of law?
5. To create agreement?
6. To solve problems? To excel? To earn a good living?
7. To do well?
8. To develop friendships?
9. To make new laws?
10. To win?
11. To be influential?
12. Other?

Where Are You Willing To Work

1. Out of my home?
2. In a rural area?
3. In suburban business district?
4. Anywhere in the U.S.?
5. Central business district?
6. In my neighborhood?
7. Foreign country?
8. Only in certain cities?

How Much Control Over Your Work Environment Do You Want

1. Owner?
2. Mid level manager?
3. Supervised employee?
4. Part of a team?
5. Freelance?
6. Senior manager?
7. Unsupervised employee?
8. Consultant?
9. Contract worker?

What Compensation Arrangement Do You Prefer
1. Salaried?
2. Contingent?
3. Incentive bonus?
4. Share of Profits?
5. Hourly?
6. Retainer?
7. Stock options?
8. Commissions?

What Size Group is Most Comfortable to You
1. By myself?
2. 5 to 15 people?
3. 41 to 150 people?
4. More than 150 people?
5. Space-sharing arrangement.

What Tasks Do You Want To Accomplish
1. Taking depositions?
2. Lead attorney in jury trials?
3. Assisting attorney in trials?
4. Negotiating?
5. Investigating?
6. Advising People?
7. Motions court Appearances?
8. Document coordinator?
9. Legal research and writing?
10. Interviewing?
11. Advising businesses?
12. Preparing witnesses?
13. Advocating positions?
14. Managing clerical staff?
15. Managing professional staff?
16. Training people?
17. Completing forms?
18. Financial analysis?

19. Law library management?
20. Drafting documents?
21. Managing cases?
22. Managing client services?
23. Lobbying?

What Subject Matter Appeals to You

1. Personal injury?
2. Domestic relations?
3. Environment law?
4. Administrative law?
5. Taxation?
6. Medical malpractice?
7. Insurance?
8. Sports?
9. Computers?
10. Poverty Law?
11. Interstate transportation?
12. Bankruptcy?
13. Civil rights?
14. Worker's compensation?
15. Creditor/debtor?
16. Health care?
17. Intellectual property?
18. Business deals?
19. Estate planning?
20. Land use planning?
21. Franchising?
22. Ethics?
23. Product liability?
24. Entertainment?
25. Patent?
26. Antitrust?
27. Utilities?
28. Banking?
29. Admiralty and maritime?

30. Woman's rights?
31. Landlord/tenant?
32. Libel and slander?
33. Securities regulation?
34. Constitutional issues?
35. Probate and guardianship?
36. Criminal prosecution or defense?
37. Law office economics?
38. Trademark and copyright?
39. Juvenile dependency?
40. Other?

Each of these questions should have allowed you to narrow down the type of law you want to practice and have expanded your idea of the types of positions available in the legal field. Go back over the questions and make a mental outline for yourself of what your ideal position would look like. In the words of Henry David Thoreau, "if one advances confidently in the direction of his dreams, and endeavors to lead the life which he has imagined, he will meet with a success unexpected in common hours." Knowing what your dream job will look like and then going for it is the only way to actually obtain it!

Conclusion

Some type of lawyer has been around since the beginning of mankind. The atmosphere and environments in law has constantly changed. There are many different types of law environments to choose to work in.

As outlined in this chapter you can choose to work in private practice, a large, medium or small law firm, corporation, government, nonprofit, educational group and prepaid legal service or as an entrepreneurs. This chapter gave you details on each environment to better enhance your ability to decide what law environment would better suit you.

You may find yourself in all of these types of settings during you career as a lawyer. Private practice and government lawyers go back and forth between the two types of employment for different periods during their career. Public service may draw you to the legal service at first, but you may use government service as the way to fulfill this need.

The advantages and disadvantages of small firm/small town vs. large firm/ large town and also the medium size firms in both large and small cities that incorporate some of the good and bad features of both have been discussed in this chapter. The choice is not an easy one and it certainly is a personal one.

You can begin the process of making decisions about your career by relating the facts in this chapter to your lifestyle choices. The type and size of the firm, the practice area, the geographic location and the attitudes of the lawyers at the firm will all have an effect on your life both at work and at home. Thus it is never too early to think about what you want out of a law firm employer and this chapter has given many helpful hints for your decision making.

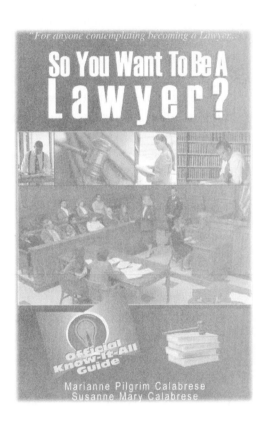

"For anyone contemplating becoming a Lawyer..."

So You Want To Be A
Lawyer?

Official Know-it-All Guide

Marianne Pilgrim Calabrese
Susanne Mary Calabrese

Chapter Four

Types of Law

Basic History of the Law

One type or another law practice has been around almost as long as mankind itself. The first legal system recorded was the Code of Hammurabi, named after the Mesopotamian ruler who adopted it about 1900BC. The code was a series of laws that defined crimes and what the punishment would be. It put society's rules in writing thus eliminating any confusion. Until then, laws were made by a ruler who could change them at will. Hammurabi's Code made sure that Mesopotamia was run according to the rule of law, a concept that became one of the most cherished principles of modern, free societies.

Law also has roots in ancient Greek and Roman times. At one time the laws were basic, and thus clearly understood by all people, effectively generating no need for lawyers. But as society became more complex so did the laws. A group of Roman aristocrats studied and developed the law. They became known as special legal advisors or juris consults. Eventually the Romans developed a more formal system with orators studying the law and presenting cases. Procurators wrote up documents and litigation began. Law schools were created with professors to teach citizens about the law. The Roman legal system spread and as a result, much of the legal profession throughout Europe has its foundation from the Romans.

After the Norman Conquest, English royal courts developed what is known as, "Common Law". Common law was mostly unwritten and was based on custom and precedent. Later, "Equity" came into practice, which was based on the dictates of conscience filling in the gaps in justice left by the common law. And later still, in the 18th century, the theory of "Natural Law" based on the natural rights of humans was stressed.

Lawyers in Literature

Shakespeare's most famous lawyer line, "The first thing we should do, let's kill all the lawyers," is not the condemnation we have come to think of it as. In fact, within the context of the play Henry VI, in Part II, (Act IV), Scene 2, it is actually an endorsement of the legal profession. The accolade is spoken by Dick the Butcher, a follower of anarchist Jack Cade, whom Shakespeare depicts as "the head of an army of rabble and a demagogue pandering to the ignorant," who sought to overthrow the government. He wanted to replace a system of laws with a dictatorship based on personal power. To Shakespeare, the rebels were a threat to order and justice, while lawyers stood in the path of anarchy. The quote actually reveals that Shakespeare was paying homage to the profession as guardians of society.

However, long before our Founding Fathers formed our legal system, Sir Thomas Moore's Uttiopia circa 1516, declared that in a utopian society, the citizens, "They have no lawyers among them for they consider them as a sort of people whose profession is to disguise matters." There has always been a love hate relationship between lawyers and society.

Lawyers in the United States

The English exported their legal system to the American Colonies. In the later years, lawyers were praised as the drafters of the Declaration of Independence and the Constitution, but they were excluded from some to the earliest American colonies. After the Revolution, lawyers became the new aristocracy after longstanding ties to the British monarchy were broken. Because of this, anti-lawyer sentiment festered from the colonial period and lawyers were in disfavor during most of the nineteenth century.

In those times any one who wanted to become a lawyer could do so by reading law books until he was ready to take an oral examination from a qualified member of the bar. The image of Abraham Lincoln studying his law books by firelight in rural Illinois and eventually parlaying his skills into a political career represents the spirit of that era of law. Other lawyers of Lincoln's period served apprenticeships to practicing lawyers, but only a small percentage were formally educated in law schools.

The first American law school, Harvard Law School opened in the United States in 1817. The standardization of the bar examination was established, the adoption of ethical codes and the evolution of strong self-regulating bar associations evolved. These changes helped to overcome contemporary negative reaction to the legal profession.

Although there is still a love hate relationship with the legal profession today, history has shown the legal profession has always maintained an important position in America society. We are a nation founded on legal principles and we frequently use lawyers to help strike the balance of power between order and liberty and between individual and state or Federal government. Lawyers have been faithful civil servants, holding positions in all branches of government: the executive legislative and judicial branches of government at the federal, state, and local level. Lawyers have been involved in every aspect of this country's growth from colonial times to present and will continue to do so.

Different Law Environments

All the different types of lawyers and their roles can work in private practice, corporations, government, non-profit, education, group and prepaid legal services and entrepreneurs. You will do most of your work in offices, law libraries, or on the computer and courtrooms. Sometimes you will meet clients in their homes or places of business and when necessary in hospitals or prisons. You have to pick the environment that will work best for you. The type of law you practice will determine where the most openings are.

Private Practice

The largest numbers of lawyers are employed in private practice where they concentrate on criminal or civil law. Instead of selling their time to one employer, private practitioners work for different clients. The private practitioners are entrepreneurs that must make enough money to run their own business. If you go into private practice you must accept the fact that law is a business and you must make a profit in order to stay in business.

There is the solo group of private practitioners; these lawyers practice alone with a legal staff. Some solo practitioners employ ten or more personnel such as paralegals, secretaries, investigators and others. If you are a good solo practitioner and businessperson you can make a good profit in this type of situation. Solo practitioners do however, statistically show the lowest per capita income of any group of attorneys.

There are benefits such as the freedom of being your own boss and making all the decisions. You will not have to answer to any other partners. You can open your business where you want. However it is difficult to be a self-employed lawyer mostly because of the significant cost of starting a new business and partly because many lawyers especially recent graduates lack the skills and experience necessary to practice competently alone. Solo practitioners have usually worked in larger firms and can network with other lawyers when the need arises.

There are many firms that are opened between family members or with groups of law school friends after a few years of private practice in a large firm. Opening your own firm is just like opening your own business – you must have your own clients in order to pay the rent and costs of doing business. If you have made a name for yourself, or if you can partner with colleagues who have well-paying clients, this is often a gamble that may pay-off very well. One large corporate client is enough to support a small firm. Starting your own firm is also a quick way to earn the title of partner, with which you can transfer laterally to other firms. The downside is that like any small business, small law firms often have a hard time paying their bills, especially since clients of lawyers are inherently more difficult to collect on-time payments from. The risk of not making a profit, the constant need to look for new clients once cases finish, and the difficulties in administrating a law firm can make this venture difficult.

Entrepreneurs go into business for themselves. They manage and market their business skills in many law areas such as real estate, commercial development, financial joint ventures, consultants and writing. If you decide to become an entrepreneur you will have to be experienced in many areas of the law with a good established networking system. You are essentially opening up your own business and you are the sole owner and worker. Often the most successful entrepreneurs have special knowledge of the law or an area of expertise that they may hire themselves out as an independent contractor. If you are considering law as a second career, you previous experience coupled with a law degree might prove very useful in this type of job.

Large, Medium and Small Law Firms

The highest paid group of private lawyers practice in large law firms. A large law firm is usually considered to have a hundred lawyers or more. They tend to be located in large cities. They usually have long-standing prestigious reputations and clients to match. These firms generally grew to such a large size to accommodate all the needs of large corporate clients' such as banks, insurance companies, industrial as well as large private estates and organizations.

Large firms tend to have the highest salaries for recent law school graduates, and for this reason competition for these positions is intense. If you do get a position in one of these firms your workload will be demanding and you will have a one in ten chance of becoming a partner. Sometimes working in a smaller branch office of a large firm offers an alternative for you to become part of the larger organization while working in an office that has the atmosphere of a smaller law firm.

A branch office is a location in a different city than the headquarters of the large firm. Most big firms have national clients and thus, have several locations across the country. Some of these offices are large, however, many of them are much smaller than others, but still have a strong connection with the other larger offices. You will be expected to work long hours including holidays. The firm will establish a goal, usually high number of billable hours that you will have to work toward each year.

Billable hours are the time that can be billed for legal service to the client. Even in small firms there may be pressure to produce billable hours. Many associates in firms work long hours for years only to be told that they will not be offered a more lucrative partnership position. Billing hours are incredibly important to the firm because they charge clients based on an hourly rate. The more time you bill a client, the more money the firm makes.

There are firms that lie in the middle of very large firms and small firms. These are firms for one reason or another that have not grown as large as their competitors or to branch out into other cities. It includes law firms that are the largest in small cities but have not opened many branches in other locations. They may be as small as fifteen or twenty lawyers or as large as fifty or hundred depending on the size of the legal needs in the city they are located. When the law firm gets somewhere between ten and twenty-five lawyers it begins to departmentalize. They subdivide along practice areas thus transforming individual practices into group practices. Medium size firms may be the remnants of other law firms that have split up in the past. Law firms are constantly changing. Small firms grow into medium and then large firms, and large firms break up into smaller ones. As a lawyer you are likely to work in several different law firms over the course of your career and even if you decide to stay in one firm it is likely you will experience a series of changes in that one firm.

The largest part of private practice is made up of small law firms. The legal profession is mostly small firm work. They are less likely to depend on large institutional clients for business. Most of these are general practices and rely on many different types of clients. There is a trend of the smaller law firms becoming more specialized. Your chances are about one in three of working for one of these types of firms during your career.

Most lawyers earn a relatively good income, however lawyers in smaller firms and in teaching positions often do not earn more than individuals with only an undergraduate education. High income is in no way guaranteed even if you are in private practice. It will depend on the ability of the firm to attract and keep clients and your ability to service them.

Corporations

If you become an in- house lawyer you may practice a variety of legal work. You will have one employer, the corporation. The largest numbers of corporate lawyers work as in- house counsels who practice law inside the corporation in a law department. Law departments can range from one or two attorneys to several hundred. The role of the department can rage from providing advice to top management, to handling legislative work, to managing outside counsel, to providing full service in house legal support. In-house law departments tend to be more hierarchical than in a small law firm. Usually one general counsel, several associate general counsels and many assistant general counsels work in a department.

Some in- house lawyers are not in any specific legal department because they supply a unique skill. They may provide legal advice to management and perform other managerial or administrative work. The companies that hire these types of lawyers are usually small. The benefit of this type of positions is that you may have an opportunity to grow with the company and eventually become the head of a growing law department.

There is also the advantage of becoming exposed to many types of law including immigration, real estate, tax and patent law. Every corporation has legal needs. The main idea of a legal department within the corporation is to pay in-house lawyers rather than expensive lawyers from an independent firm in order to lower their legal fees. Most of the time, in-house lawyers save the corporation a lot of money in legal costs. An attorney in a small corporation may have responsibilities other then the legal affairs. Some corporations hire new lawyers to handle legal problems and assume management duties too. A practice in a corporation provides a diversity of experiences for lawyers but it may prove to be an incredibly stressful position as well.

If you become an in- house corporate lawyer you will probably have a better salary then in a law firm. Fringe benefits like mobility, insurance, employee saving plans and. retirement also tend to be better in corporations because even small businesses tend to employ more people then large law firms. Corporations may offer stock options or other financial incentives as well, that a law firm would not.

When you compare large and small corporate law departments there are some significant differences. In a large corporation the company operations may be so diverse that you may have the feeling that you are working for a number of clients. You usually specialize as a lawyer in a large corporation and you may have a practice that is much closer to that of a lawyer in a large law firm than a lawyer in a small firm. The practice in a small corporate law department may be more like that in a small firm where you will be expected to do a myriad of different tasks for one client. The benefit is that you will have the opportunity to gain valuable experience and grow with the company. Often where there are fewer people to perform the many tasks necessary in a case, an inexperienced lawyer will be given more meaningful responsibility at a smaller firm.

The corporate law department may offer some unusual opportunities for a junior attorney. Generally, corporations don't even look at new law graduates because they don't have the resources to train new lawyers. Most companies won't look at an applicant who doesn't have at least 3 years experience. You may likely be more closely involved in the running of the business, in such things as determining policy and becoming involved in management. In a big company you may have a feeling of being isolated from the action, or not understanding how one's work actually fits into the organization. This can be frustrating to someone who needs to see the results of her or his work.

The large size corporate giants can offer some fringe benefits. If you are unhappy in one department there is a good possibility you can transfer to another. If you want to travel there are likely opportunities to transfer to a department more well suited to your needs. For example, some corporations may even enable you to enter the field of international law. In many corporations, experienced lawyers fill the overseas positions while the new lawyers may find themselves doing the international practice in law libraries in domestic law offices.

Corporate law departments are growing rapidly and they are using the law school graduate to meet their employment needs. It is clear that practice in a corporation is a viable career path in the legal profession today.

Government

Government positions give lawyers two important assets, expertise in a particular field of law and contacts that may lead to clients in private practices. The government agencies where you can work are federal, military, state, judicial, city, and quasi-governmental. Government position can give you more security and better working hours than private practice. But the financial rewards are usually a lot less.

If you want to work for the federal government, it is the largest government service. The positions tend to be in Washington D.C. The United Stated Law Department is the largest law firm in the world; it has one client, the United States. Most of the work is litigation within the many divisions. The Internal Revenue Service also employs a large number of lawyers with special training in taxes and accounting. Also there is the United States District Court a branch of the United States Attorney office.

The military also hires civilian and military lawyers. Primarily lawyers are in the military Judge Advocate General's Corp or JAG. These officers are usually recruited straight from law school or sometimes sent to law school in return for a commitment to work at JAG. If you work in this department you can serve on military agencies around the world, representing service men and women in cases form court martial to disputes involving civilian issues. You can also be a civil lawyer in areas such government contracts.

State governments have many departments like the federal government. All states have an attorney general office, tax division, education department and other components. If you work for a state government the issues will be more localized and you may have opportunities for positions in administration, as hearing officers and research analysis.

In the judicial branch of government, lawyers can serve as judges, law clerks and judicial administrators. Most judges are experienced and respected lawyers. Law clerking will give you the opportunity to learn the judicial system by working for a judge, conducting research, and completing many other forms of assistance. These positions provide you with excellent credentials to further your career and are highly coveted.

Local government lawyers usually function like in house lawyers, of course this depends on the size of the local government. Usually separate departments represent the city or county in civil matters and prosecute violations of the law in stare or local courts. Also legal positions with many local boards and authorities are available.

The quasi-governmental work includes agencies that constitute joint ventures between the public and the private sector. If you like politics and want to eventually run for office a government law position may be for you.

Nonprofit Law

The Legal Services Corporation provides legal services to Americans who cannot otherwise afford representation. These law positions are usually government-funded positions. Other forms of nonprofit law are specific political action, law reform, and public interest groups. America has become a nation of interest groups, and nonprofits have become more and more important. These include private organizations, professional associations, citizen watchdog groups, campaign fund raising committees, religious groups and benevolent organizations.

Education

Lawyers are employed in all levels of education. As a lawyer you can work as a college professor high school teacher, primary educator, administrative agent or school district counselor. You can also present workshops, speak for education programs and host information seminars. It is also possible to supplement your position in private practice with a teaching position. Not only does this improve your resume and vastly increase your academic resources, it can greatly improve your networking with other prominent attorneys that are often on the faculty.

Group and Prepaid Legal Services

Group legal services can be compared to medical HMO while prepaid legal services resemble medical insurance. They were developed to provide affordable legal services to the middle class. Group legal services are often provided through some trade or professional association such as a union. If you work as a lawyer in this type of atmosphere you most likely will work for an independent private practitioner and the form of pay will vary. Under a prepaid plan, clients would be reimbursed for legal expenses and selects the lawyers of their choice. These types of plans have not been widely used by the general public.

How to Find an Environment That Will Satisfy Your Needs

The following questions will help you target the type of legal work that most appeals to you. Before you answer each questions, make sure you are responding to your own feelings and not to what you believe would most impress others or meet the expectations of your family, friends, or colleagues. When you have answered all the questions, and have a clearer vision of your preferences, incorporate the answers into a description of your ideal legal position. Then begin to research the job market to locate jobs that fit that description.

What Are Your Work Values?
1. To help people?
2. To help businesses?
3. To meet intellectual challenges?
4. To study thoroughly points of law?
5. To create agreement?
6. To solve problems? To excel? To earn a good living?
7. To do well?
8. To develop friendships?
9. To make new laws?
10. To win?
11. To be influential?
12. Other?

Where Are You Willing To Work
1. Out of my home?
2. In a rural area?
3. In suburban business district?
4. Anywhere in the U.S.?
5. Central business district?
6. In my neighborhood?
7. Foreign country?
8. Only in certain cities?

How Much Control Over Your Work Environment Do You Want
1. Owner?
2. Mid level manager?
3. Supervised employee?
4. Part of a team?
5. Freelance?
6. Senior manager?
7. Unsupervised employee?
8. Consultant?
9. Contract worker?

What Compensation Arrangement Do You Prefer
1. Salaried?
2. Contingent?
3. Incentive bonus?
4. Share of Profits?
5. Hourly?
6. Retainer?
7. Stock options?
8. Commissions?

What Size Group is Most Comfortable to You
1. By myself?
2. 5 to 15 people?
3. 41 to 150 people?
4. More than 150 people?
5. Space-sharing arrangement.

What Tasks Do You Want To Accomplish
1. Taking depositions?
2. Lead attorney in jury trials?
3. Assisting attorney in trials?
4. Negotiating?
5. Investigating?
6. Advising People?
7. Motions court Appearances?
8. Document coordinator?
9. Legal research and writing?
10. Interviewing?
11. Advising businesses?
12. Preparing witnesses?
13. Advocating positions?
14. Managing clerical staff?
15. Managing professional staff?
16. Training people?
17. Completing forms?
18. Financial analysis?

19. Law library management?
20. Drafting documents?
21. Managing cases?
22. Managing client services?
23. Lobbying?

What Subject Matter Appeals to You

1. Personal injury?
2. Domestic relations?
3. Environment law?
4. Administrative law?
5. Taxation?
6. Medical malpractice?
7. Insurance?
8. Sports?
9. Computers?
10. Poverty Law?
11. Interstate transportation?
12. Bankruptcy?
13. Civil rights?
14. Worker's compensation?
15. Creditor/debtor?
16. Health care?
17. Intellectual property?
18. Business deals?
19. Estate planning?
20. Land use planning?
21. Franchising?
22. Ethics?
23. Product liability?
24. Entertainment?
25. Patent?
26. Antitrust?
27. Utilities?
28. Banking?
29. Admiralty and maritime?

30. Woman's rights?
31. Landlord/tenant?
32. Libel and slander?
33. Securities regulation?
34. Constitutional issues?
35. Probate and guardianship?
36. Criminal prosecution or defense?
37. Law office economics?
38. Trademark and copyright?
39. Juvenile dependency?
40. Other?

Each of these questions should have allowed you to narrow down the type of law you want to practice and have expanded your idea of the types of positions available in the legal field. Go back over the questions and make a mental outline for yourself of what your ideal position would look like. In the words of Henry David Thoreau, "if one advances confidently in the direction of his dreams, and endeavors to lead the life which he has imagined, he will meet with a success unexpected in common hours." Knowing what your dream job will look like and then going for it is the only way to actually obtain it!

Conclusion

Some type of lawyer has been around since the beginning of mankind. The atmosphere and environments in law has constantly changed. There are many different types of law environments to choose to work in.

 As outlined in this chapter you can choose to work in private practice, a large, medium or small law firm, corporation, government, nonprofit, educational group and prepaid legal service or as an entrepreneurs. This chapter gave you details on each environment to better enhance your ability to decide what law environment would better suit you.

You may find yourself in all of these types of settings during you career as a lawyer. Private practice and government lawyers go back and forth between the two types of employment for different periods during their career. Public service may draw you to the legal service at first, but you may use government service as the way to fulfill this need.

The advantages and disadvantages of small firm/small town vs. large firm/ large town and also the medium size firms in both large and small cities that incorporate some of the good and bad features of both have been discussed in this chapter. The choice is not an easy one and it certainly is a personal one.

You can begin the process of making decisions about your career by relating the facts in this chapter to your lifestyle choices. The type and size of the firm, the practice area, the geographic location and the attitudes of the lawyers at the firm will all have an effect on your life both at work and at home. Thus it is never too early to think about what you want out of a law firm employer and this chapter has given many helpful hints for your decision making.

Chapter Five

Meet the Lawyers

This is the chapter that gives you examples of the personalities of lawyers and their lives. There are many different types of lawyers just as there are many different types of people. Certain personality traits and skills lend themselves better to certain types of law and working environments. If you are in a large law firm you will find the personalities of your colleagues will affect you more than if you had your own business.

If you have an independent nature, are ambitious and like to make your own decision you may find that starting your own law firm is right for you. Or maybe you like the security of a large firm where you will receive a steady income, better benefits and a larger pool of resources comprised of your peers, senior lawyers and staff. Maybe doing the work that makes you feel good will give you the most satisfaction, then maybe public interest law is for you. Either way you will have to learn the personalities of the lawyers that you work with in order to successfully interact with them.

In this chapter you will be introduced to different types of lawyers, their personalities and the career decisions they made. Their stories may help you find your best place in the law field.

The Do The Right Thing Lawyer

Bill is a thirty-year-old man who always knew he wanted to go to law school and become a criminal lawyer. He works as a public prosecutor. He feels there is no field of law more important than criminal law. It has life and death consequences and that's why he likes it.
He majored in psychology in college and this background has helped him

learn how people think. He recommends this major to anyone thinking about going to law school. Bill decided to go into the public sector because he wanted to get some basic experience before he went into his own practice. But while he was working as a prosecutor he discovered something about himself. He discovered he didn't need a large salary and he did not practice just for the money. Although he is still making a decent salary by his standards, he could be making a lot more in private practice. He stayed in this job because he likes being part of "doing the right thing".

The right thing for him is making sure people who are a threat to law abiding citizens get locked up for a good long time. He feels he knows how to tell a real criminal from a decent kid who made a bad decision. He prides himself in that he can make deals with small time crooks and get information that will help bring the big time criminals to justice. He likes being on the cutting edge of the criminal justice system every day.

Since he is only thirty and not married, he feels he has plenty of time to go into private practice someday, if he still wants to. Making the switch from prosecutor to defense attorney would be relatively easy because of his experience. He's not sure he would ever want to defend some of the criminals he's seen, but he feels he is a good lawyer and could represent his clients to the best of his ability - no matter who that client happens to be.

High Income Lawyer

Sam works in a large law firm with over 850 lawyers. It is a tax controversy firm, so all the lawyers, including Sam, are tax attorneys. Sam's main incentive for working in this firm is to make money; some of the partners earn over $1 million a year. He wants to become a partner and earn a similar salary. He has dreams of owning his own yacht and sailing around the world. When Sam graduated from law school, he was interested in the field of labor law, but then switched to this firm shortly thereafter. He actually had no courses in taxation when he switched. All of his expertise he learned from case work and other attorneys.

He has been working in the firm for five years. He works long days and works about sixty hours or more a week, but he earns a substantial salary. The long hours are hard on his wife and two children. He has a nice house, a nice vacation house, prestige cars and his kids will be able to go to any college they can get into. The negative side is that sometimes the only quality time he gets to spend with his family is when they go on vacation and even his vacations are interrupted by work

He is a very intelligent, sociable man with great writing and oral skills who knows everything about the tax laws. He likes the challenges and he accomplishes a lot through negotiation. The work is never boring, which helps when working long hours. Often he has worked on big cases with well-known clients. But he made a lot of sacrifices to get where he is and he will make more to become a partner. Sometimes he is afraid he may burn out before he becomes a partner and considers moving to a position at another firm which requires less hours, but for now he loves his work. He feels underneath it all he never lost sight of what it means to be a lawyer and he is achieving his goal of making a lot of money.

Control of Own Practice

Maggie is an independent young woman with strong ideals and beliefs of her own. She wanted to go to law school ever since she was in third grade. At her state college, she excelled and then headed straight to law school. While in law school, she worked at her State Attorney's General's Office as a clerk. As part of her job, she went to various courts and observed how other lawyers were handling their cases. She made a lot of contacts there that helped her get clients later.

Eventually she decided to open her own law practice. She started out with "space for service" which was a little desk in an office with other lawyers. She provided some services in payment for her space such as going to court or looking up information. She had many lean months where she wasn't making much profit, but finally was able to rent her own office in a building where other lawyers had offices. She had never worked in a law firm where she could learn from experienced lawyers and this was proving to be a disadvantage. While in the large office building, she befriended many experienced lawyers around her and learned a great deal.

She became involved in the New York Bar Association Committee, which teamed her up with an experienced lawyer who helped her learn more about the practice of law. She also joined several Bar Associations and became active on a number of committees. She attended seminars and listened to speakers.

In the beginning of her career she handled virtually everything, bankruptcies, collections, divorces, personal injury, wills, mortgages and real estate closings. As time went on she became more and more involved with divorce work. She now usually starts her day going directly to divorce court for motions, seeking child support, temporary custody or evicting a spouse. On other days she will meet clients in her office to review what will happen in court.

She some times puts in fourteen-hour days. She feels she really has to put the time in to do well. Her firm now grosses over $400,000 a year. She is the only lawyer and she is in control of her own firm. She recently hired two people, an assistant and a paralegal. She is glad she had the power and control to hire them and they seemed to be working out. She is not married; she says she is married to her profession. She loves what she does and loves having control over her personal as well as professional life.

Another solo-practicing lawyer is Mark. He has a staff of two legal secretaries, one paralegal and a receptionist. He is very respectful of his all women staff and knows how to work with them for the best results. He will ask them to make corrections in a presentable manner and explains everything in an understanding, practical way. His staff has been with him for a long time. They enjoy working for him and respect the treatment and fellow comradeship in the office. He is a personable, informative man who makes his clients and staff feel at ease and confidant with his work. His law office handles mostly personal injury cases and he boasts he handles about one hundred and twenty five cases at a time. A client can go to him for any type of business. For example, you can have a reasonable priced will made out and he spends many hours with you in order to get it done effectively and to your liking. He can afford to be reasonably priced because he lives in a state where the cost of living is low and he reflects his prices accordingly. He is proud of his accomplishments and acknowledges that he could not have accomplished this alone, so he is grateful and proud of his staff.

He started out working for a large firm but found the hours and the politics not to his liking. He is a family man and takes pride in his wife, children and grandchildren. He likes having the freedom of making his own hours so he can spend time with his family. Mark has found a balance life while working in the legal profession and now he is enjoying the contentment of his work.

Make a Difference Lawyer

Jeff is an in-house corporate lawyer. He is a logical thinker with the ability to clearly communicate his ideas. He is extremely passionate about his work and he feels he helps and makes a difference in his company. He was always interested in business and he feels it stems from his family running their own business. As a child he lived and breathed the family business.

After law school he worked in a variety of situations. He tried a small law firm and then he eventually became a partner in a large firm. He also worked for a federal agency and a trade association before he began working as an in- house lawyer for a private company. He was never afraid to try different things in the legal profession and he learned from every position he ever had. As an associate he worked long hours producing 1900 to 2000 billable hours a year. As he moved up the firm, his billable hours, decreased, but there were increasing administrative responsibilities. Thus, his time devoted to the firm never decreased. He worked evening and weekends for the firm and worked after 6 PM many days. This lifestyle took a toll on his family life. He decided to switch positions to a Company where fewer hours were required of him. It has worked out very well. Jeff still makes an excellent salary, but has more regulated hours which allows him to spend time with his family.

He does a lot of Bar association work and feels it boosts his career as well as keeps him up-to-date on matters affecting his practice. He has gotten to know lawyers in other cities through the Bar association and finds this very rewarding both personally and professionally. The Bar association helps him continue his legal education by sharpening his skills and developing his reputation. He participates in panels and demonstrates his knowledge in a positive way.

He tries to have a personal relationship with his client while providing advice and knowledge. He accomplishes building trust on an intimate level while helping to avoid the pitfalls of businesses. He keeps up with the current business laws and feels it is a lifelong learning process. . Because of the speed at which law can be practiced due to electronic communication, Jeff sometimes feels he is under pressure to act immediately and may make a mistake in doing so. He tries to tell associates that even though more information is available on the Internet, you cannot make legal recommendations instantaneously. You need to consider carefully the implication of changes in documents and contracts. Jeff reads and analyzes things thoroughly before he presents them to the client to ensure the right thing for his client.

Back to Roots lawyer

Marie comes from a large family and knows what it means to be poor. She put herself through college and then law school. First she went into environmental law. She really thought it would be fulfilling, but somehow her interest in the environment never matched what she did in her actual law practice. Her career in environmental law did not give her the satisfaction she was after, so she decided it was time to go back to her roots. She now works for a nonprofit law group that helps migrant worker with their basic rights. She also deals with local employment matters. In this, she finally found the satisfaction she was looking for.

She thoroughly enjoys what she does. The clients really need her help and they are very grateful when they get positive results. Many of her clients remind her of her parents when they first came to this country. She speaks Spanish fluently, and that helps greatly when dealing with her clients. She does a lot of work out of the office, in the fields, in the factories - basically wherever the workers are. She likes that part of her job; she couldn't stand working at a desk all day. She loves the people she works with and she is happy that there isn't any of the negative office politics that existed at some of the other firms she worked for.

he is very involved in the community and knows most of the people personally who need her help. This provides her with the opportunity to be with people whose company she enjoys, while helping them with her knowledge of law. She likes this setting better than the business environment that comes with most law positions.

She doesn't get paid what she could be if she was working in a larger private firm, but then she doesn't have to defend cases or companies she doesn't believe in either. Her income is adequate for her. She is used to living on a lot less. She will put in long days when it is necessary but then has ample time off to enjoy with her husband and daughter. She doesn't have to work 60 or 70-hour weeks that she would have if she were at another firm. She feels that she has a balanced life. With the gratification she gets from her clients, she can't see doing anything else.

Compassionate Lawyer

Jane is glad she chose employment law. She likes it because it doesn't have the hostile clients she saw in family law or the seedy clients she saw in criminal law. Basically she feels she works with good people who have been wronged and she really feels compassion for her clients. Her clients are hurt, angry, and sometimes defeated by what happen to them in the workplace. Not only is she an attorney, but she is often a counselor and a support person for them. When she wins a case, and gets someone their job back, fair wages, or changes a negative work environment, she feels worthwhile and that clients have been compensated for their trouble.

At her firm, she is an associate who mostly does work for two partners, although there are about 20 other attorneys in the office. She generally likes the two partners, but is sometimes annoyed by the constant interruptions to her work by one of the partners who often gives her assignments. At this point, she is mostly a draft lawyer who drafts pleadings, settlements, contracts and court required documents. The other part of her day is spent on the phone with clients. Two years ago when she began at this firm, she was earning $50,000. That was lower than some other positions she was offered in other areas, but she is happy she is working and gaining experience in employment law.

She works in a medium sized city in a medium sized firm. She is a member of a Women Lawyers group and enjoys participating in the local bar association activities. The interaction with other lawyers helps her greatly. She finds employment laws and regulations intricate and is challenged by figuring out the right way to approach a case. It is stressful at times, because of the tough corporate adversaries, but she has learned to let her frustrations go when she gets home. She has learned not to let her job become all consuming in her thoughts. It's a big part of her life but she wants to make her family more important to her. She has three children and a husband she wants to spend more time with and has been trying to work fewer hours to be at home more.

Engineer Turned Lawyer

Jim has a degree in mechanical engineering and law. He became interested in the laws governing patents when he tried to get a patent application for an invention. Because of his outstanding grades and work, several law firms, recruited him. He decided on a firm that had a good mix of corporate law along with an outstanding reputation. He passed the bar examine on his first try and at the suggestion of his bosses decided to get some in-house experience before taking the patent bar examination. It is a difficult exam and, like the bar, he took a review course to help him pass it.

His work is very complex and challenging, He advises clients mainly in manufacturing, if their proposed invention is novel, workable, and saleable in comparison to other like patent in the particular area. He understands what the client is trying to accomplish with the invention and how and why it works. His mechanical engineering degree and experience provides him with the necessary knowledge to be able to make a technical evaluation on whether a patent application should be filed.

He loves his work, but sometimes he knows clients can have unrealistic expectations about their ideas and creations and expect miracles from him in obtaining patents or other protective devices. He knows he will be perceived as negative if he says that the ideas are not workable, too costly to produce, or too similar to another patented product or service. Clients have sued him over this. This aspect of the work is very frustrating and he still thinks about the clients that wrongly sued him.

He does his work very carefully and he does a great deal of research before a decision is made to apply for a patent. He works with patent agents and other patent lawyers. Some patent agents have scientific technical backgrounds that help in the investigation he does of the technical field involved. He then drafts a patent application complete with detailed descriptions of how the invention is made and used, including diagrams and drawings, a set of claims that define what the invention can do and the inventor' patents rights. The application is then filed with the US Patent and Trademark Office in Washington and is assigned to a patent examiner.

The whole process can take months or even years. There is always more investigation, amendments to the original claims, and other matters to negotiate. He has numerous conversations and meetings in order to plan his strategies. When he is successful, his client get a patent giving them the right to exclude all others from making, using and selling the invention in the United States for the next 20 years. If the application is denied then he appeals and can continue in the US court of Appeals for the Federal Circuit.

He says he is very happy as a patent lawyer. He finds the work interesting and challenging and he makes a good salary. He intends to start a family soon and wants to have time to enjoy them.

Never Can Please Lawyer

Jean is a partner in a small law firm where she has been working forever. She comes in early in the morning and doesn't leave till late at night. No one in the office really knows very much about her personal life, she never shares that sort of information. She asks paralegal and secretaries to do work in an impatient manner. She explains the work to them quickly and answers any question in a curt way. Then, she gets upset if they don't do it to her liking.

You can hear her talk about the inefficient secretaries in the office to her fellow lawyers. When a new associate came to the office she was polite in an anxious sort of way. She is friendly only with the older original lawyer of the small firm and you can find her in his office talking about the new associates and other workers. She will very rarely go out and socialize with any of the other lawyers in the office.

The small law firm is growing and she had a lot to do with this. She knows how to bring in clients and is very efficient in pleasing them and getting referrals. The older partner knows this and tries to keep her happy. He assigns her new secretaries and paralegal hoping that one will please her. He quietly moves or lets go a secretary that isn't to her liking with a little apology and severance pay. The new associates stay out of her way and hope they do not have to work with her She usually works alone unless there is a big case that just can't be handled by one lawyer and then the older original lawyer will usually work with her.

Royalty lawyer

Charles is the head equity partner of a large law firm in a large city. He has been at the firm since he graduated from law school and came up through the ranks. He is a very precise person. Everything is done to perfection and in a neatly organized manner. He expects the same from his staff. He has gone through more secretaries than any one else in the company. He finally found one that kind of meets his criteria and she has been with him for five years. She sharpens his pencils brings him his coffee, says whatever he instructs her to say to family, friends, and clients over the phone and does what ever it takes to keep him happy. Everyone calls her the angel in the office, because when he is happy the office is happy.

He has been known to have a temper tantrum from time to time, which embarrasses his fellow colleagues and staff. At one time or another he has been seen screaming at a new associate. The new associates quickly learn to stay out of his way and not to work with him if possible. The unfortunate associates who need to work with him soon learn to go through his secretary who can be a buffer and make it possible to work with him.

He will socialize with his fellow partners and goes out with them after work. That is how he met his third wife. He brings in a great deal of money to the firm and his co- partners appreciate this. None of them ever talk to him about his behavior; they just give him what he wants. If he doesn't like the associate he is working with a new one is assigned to him.

Conclusion

These are embellishments of some of the personalities of lawyers you might find in any law environment. Many lawyers have a few of each of these personality traits In any large law firm there will be the, Do the Right Thing Lawyer, who wants to make sure people who are a threat to society get put in prison, or the High Income Lawyer, who is making and want to make that enormous salary. Then you will find the independent personality who wants to run their own law firm and knows how to make it succeed. There are the lawyers want to grow with a company and make a difference for their clients. The Back to Roots Lawyer personality enables him or her to go back to their formative years and help make right what they lived through. Then there are the compassionate lawyers who make it their quest to help their client.

When you start a new position in a law firm it will take just a few weeks to assess the various personalities of the lawyer's that you encounter. You can learn from each lawyer's personality. For yourself, choose to highlight the good traits that will help you achieve your own personal goals. Key in on what personality traits are not working and avoid falling into the same traps. Find what personality traits work best in different situation and pattern yourself from that.

Most lawyers are within the normal personality range and will be helpful to you if you know how to interact with them. One or two might be dangerous to your position. Use each personality to your best advantage and find the best traits to help you ease into the legal profession. Select the environment where you have the best chance of being treated the best for success.

"For anyone contemplating becoming a Lawyer..."

So You Want To Be A
Lawyer?

Official
Know-It-All
Guide

Marianne Pilgrim Calabrese
Susanne Mary Calabrese

Chapter Six

Salaries and Opportunities

As a lawyer you will have opportunities to live and work in numerous places and areas. You can work in large cities, small cities, and towns or in rural areas. Also you will have an opportunity to work for a large, medium or small law firms, corporations, government agencies or go into private practice. The type of law you want to practice will also affect your opportunities and salary in the legal profession.

You must realistically accept that you are going to have to do a little work and make some sacrifices in order to get a law position. In order to find a position you may have to relocate and be willing to try different types of law. 88% of lawyers practice in large cities and more than half work in private practice. The most popular cities are New York, Los Angeles, Washington, D.C. and Chicago. New York has been the nation's largest legal hub.

The most prestigious positions are few and far between and are achieved only after intense competitions. You have about a 20% chance of working in a law firm of over 100 lawyers and less of a chance of getting a prestigious judicial clerkship position. You have more of a chance of getting into private practice. In the legal profession, as in any career, getting your first job is often about whom you know not what you know. First go through all your connections. Contact everyone you know in the legal profession and see what they can do for you.

Lawyers held about 695,000 jobs in 2002. About 3 out of 4 lawyers practiced privately, either in law firms or in solo practices. Most of the remaining lawyers held positions in government or with corporations or nonprofit organizations.

For those working in government, the greatest numbers were employed at the local level. Lawyers who work for state attorney's general, prosecutors, public defenders, and courts play a key role in the criminal justice system. At the Federal level, attorneys investigate cases for the U.S. Department of Justice and other agencies. Government lawyers also help develop programs, draft and interpret laws and legislation, establish enforcement procedures and argue civil and criminal cases on behalf of the government.

Employment opportunities for lawyers should grow about as fast as the average career through 2012, because of growth in the population and in basic business activities. Demand will increase for legal services in areas as elder, antitrust, environmental, and intellectual property law. There should also be an increase in use of legal services by the middle class because of wider availability and affordability of legal clinics and prepaid legal service programs.

Growth will continue to be in salaried jobs, as businesses and all levels of government employ a growing number of staff attorneys and as employment in the legal services industry grows. The number of self-employed lawyers is expected to decrease slowly, reflecting the difficulty of establishing a profitable new practice with the competition from large, established law firms.

You may have considerable debt when you graduate law school yet there is no guarantee you will quickly find a position. There are almost a million lawyers in the United States. About 38,000 students graduate every year from 200 law schools in the United States. The competition is very keen for jobs and clients. Obviously, economic conditions affect the number of jobs available. During recessions, demand declines for some legal services, such as planning estates, drafting wills, and handling real estate transactions. Also some corporate law departments may hire only experienced lawyers and are less likely to litigate cases in- house. On the other hand individual and corporations face other legal problems, such as bankruptcies, foreclosures and divorces requiring legal assistance.

There are many things you can do to better your chances of getting a position in law. The first is to acknowledge that you are going to have to do a little work and make some sacrifice to get a position. You may have to accept a position in areas outside of your field of interest or for which you feel overqualified. Maybe you will have to do temporary staffing work, where they will place you in a temporary job, until you are able to secure a full time position. Where you live, if you are willing to relocate, your choice of specialty, and the environment where you work will help you find and get a law position. Also, finding a summer internship during law school may often assure you a job at that firm when you graduate.

Salaries, Billable Hours and Contingencies

Most lawyers make a nice living but they don't become rich. The few lawyers who do become rich are few and far between and most acquire their wealth from other business. Lawyers may work for the wealthy but they don't become wealthy practicing law. You can expect to make a comfortable living as a lawyer but you probably will not be rich.

Many things influence the salaries offered to new law graduates, academic record, type, size and location of employer and the specialized educational background desired. The type of law also will determine the salary. As an example, Patent lawyers generally receive the highest salaries.

In 2002, the median annual earnings of all lawyers were $90,290. The middle half of the occupation earned between $61,060 and $136,810. The lowest paid 10 percent earned less than $44,490; at least 10 percent earned more than $145,600. Median annual earnings in the industries employing the largest numbers of lawyers in 2002 were management of companies and enterprises $131,970, federal government $98,790, legal services $93,970, local government $69,710 and state government $67,910.

Lawyers' median salary, six months after graduation from law school in 2001 varied by type of work. Lawyers in private practice earned $90,000, business/industry earned $60,000, judicial clerkship and government $40,300, and academe $40,000

Salaries of experienced attorneys vary widely according to the type, size, and location of their employer. Lawyers who own their own practices usually earn less than those who are partners in law firms. Lawyers starting their own practice may need to work part time in other occupations to supplement their income until their practice is well established.

Salaried lawyers usually have structured work schedules. Lawyers in private practice may work irregular hours while conducting research, conferring with clients, or preparing briefs during non-office hours. If you are a salaried lawyer you obviously receive increases according to your level of responsibility. Most salaried lawyers are provided with health and life insurance, and contributions are made on their behalf to retirement plans. Lawyers who practice independently are covered only if they arrange and pay for such benefits themselves.

You may find yourself in a position where you have to track billable hours in order to get paid. This means you will have to write down which client should be billed for each hour or fraction of an hour of time that you spent working. Compensation and evaluation is based on the billable hours. In many law firms each lawyer is expected to put in a specific number of billable hours per week.

Some lawyers work on contingency rather then on an hourly fee or salaried. If you work on contingency you will get a percentage of the money received when the case is closed. This can be very good or very bad depending on how your cases do. Even if you win it may take years to settle a case and get the money.

Law position will probably continue to be concentrated in salaried jobs, because businesses and all levels of government employ a growing number of staff attorneys and employment in the legal services in industry is growing. Most salaried positions are in urban areas where government agencies, law firms, and big corporations are concentrated.

The number of self-employed lawyers is expected to decrease slowly, reflecting the difficulty of establishing a profitable new practice in the face of competition from larger, established law firms. Moreover, the growing complexity of law, which encourages specialization, along with the cost of maintaining up-to-date legal research materials, favors larger firms.

Three Most Important Factors

You have to decide what is most important to you. Is it where you live or the type of law you practice or the setting where you work? If living in a big city is a must for you then where you work and what type of law you practice may have to be compromised in order to stay in a city. There are three main things you have to prioritize when looking for a position. They are;

1. Where you live, big city, small city, town or rural area,
2. Where you work, large , medium or small firm, government office, solo practice or small partnership company
3. The type of law you want to go into and the way you will earn your income in these positions .

Which is the most important to you? Which one has to come first to satisfy your needs? Decide now which comes first, second and third. Where do you really want to live, what type of setting would you be most happy working in and is it the most important factor for you? Is how you get paid the essential thing you must think about? Did you go into law to practice a certain type of law, which you absolutely must do in order to be fulfilled.

One factor may just stick out and you know that is the most important thing. If you are not sure which one is the most important then take a piece of paper, separate it into the three categories, Where you live, Where you work and What type of law and salary, and write down all the reasons each factor is important to you. The list that is the longest will probably be the factor that is most important to you.

Now that you have put them in the proper order you can logically go about finding the best position. If working in a particular type of law was you first choice then go to the law firms etc. and areas where there is the most need and openings in that type of law. If you must work for a large law firm in a salaried position then apply to large law firms around the country. You will find a position if you are willing to compromise in at least one or maybe two of these three factors.

Where You Live

The five states with the largest population of lawyers are California, New York, Texas, Florida and Illinois. One out of ten Americans lives in California and one out of four live in the other states. California seems to have a larger proportion of lawyers than the average population in that state maybe because of the high numbers of law schools in California. Lawyers tend to stay and practice in the state they go to school in. The northeast area between Boston and Washington DC is a favorite area for lawyers to work in.

Large Cities, Small Cities, Towns and Rural Areas

Of course large cities provide you with the most opportunities. You can find work in any type of law or setting in a large city. The competition is also steep in a large city. You have to be willing to live in a city and like that lifestyle. The city is where you will have the greatest opportunity to earn the highest salary and practice whatever type of law you desire.

You can work for the largest law firm where there will be hundreds of lawyers or have a solo practice in a large city. While there are ample opportunities there is also a lot of competition for jobs, clients, and business in general. It is also where you will find the most intense type of law practice. You may find it hard to get a position in a large city even with all the opportunities. If this occurs consider relocating

There are opportunities in small cities and towns as well. These areas may have colleges, industries or military installations. They may be on an important crossroad or market like Natchez, Mississippi or Lancaster, Pennsylvania. There, locals Bar Associations are usually smaller and more likely to be cohesive because everyone will probably know each other. If you wish to establish your own practice it will probably be easier to do in a small town or expanding suburban area. In these communities, competition from large established law firms is likely to be less than in a big city and new lawyers may find it easier to become known to clients.

A large law firm in a small city or town may have 10 or 15 lawyers. You may have the pleasure of a short commute to work. The law practice may not be as intense as in a larger city or financially as rewarding but the slower pace and more family oriented style may be attractive to you.

Some law school graduates find it hard to get accepted in a small town or city if they do not have any family roots there. If you are willing to devote the time and effort to break through the social barriers the opportunities can be very beneficial. This life style may not be for everyone but for many it is worth giving up the bright lights and big city life for. If you want a quiet kind of life and have lived or want to live in a smaller community this might be the place for you.

Rural area's industries are usually farming, ranching, logging, fishing, etc. and the law that you will be practicing will image these things. The bar associations in these rural areas are small and intimate with sometimes only 10 to 20 lawyers. Some say that law gets done more quickly and efficiently in these rural areas than in the big cities. Cases may be settled over coffee and a lawyer's word is considered his bond. Your income will most likely be a lot less then if you worked in any kind of city, and the legal work itself may be average and routine. Everyone will know everything about you and you will know everything about them. You have to take into consideration the lack of cultural stimulation you might encounter in rural areas but there will be other means of enjoyment.

However there is a great need for lawyers in rural areas and this might be a good opportunity for you if you are used to this lifestyle or would like to get used to this lifestyle. You also have to consider getting accepted by the rural community. This may take some time and effort, but it can be very rewarding.

One of the main things you have to realize if you decide to become a lawyer is that you may have to relocate to get the job you want. If you find yourself an unemployed law school graduate it is probably not because there are no positions but rather there are no positions in the area you are in. There are too many lawyers in some areas and not enough in others.

Types of Legal Services

There are basically three sections of the law that will help you know where your opportunities lie. There is the general population, the government section, and the business market. An area may have a greater or fewer number of lawyers depending on the needs in that area. The general population may need certain types of lawyers depending on age, income and individual legal problems of the population in that area. Government practice depends on the amount and kind of government agencies in the area. Legal needs of business can vary widely depending on where and what the business deals with.

Many factors affect these areas and the demand for legal services. Some factors may help to increase demands for your services. Think about the following steps and how you can incorporate them into your practice to make yourself more marketable:

1. Bring services to groups who have been under represented, such as immigrants, underprivileged and middle class in certain areas.
2. Specialize in new types of law such as computer law

3. Do teaching and judicially work
4. Relocating to rural areas
5. Take a position that was in the past held by a non lawyer
6. Becoming an expert in local business affairs
7. Find what the population in your area needs in the way of legal services and learn to do it
8. Find what government sectors need law services

The type of law you want to practice will determine where and what setting you most likely will find a position in. For example, if you want to work in public interest law then you will have to go where these types of positions are. (Usually in Washington DC   working in a salaried position at a government. agency.) Maybe you don't have a specialty of law in mind. Then you will have a wider field of positions to choose from. You can develop your skills to meet the needs and job opportunities.

You may have to accept a position in areas outside of your field of interest or for which you feel overqualified. If you are unable to find a permanent position try a temporary staffing firm. These firms will place you in a short-term lawyer position until you are able to secure a full-time job. This service allows companies to hire you on an "as-needed" basis and permits beginning lawyers to develop practical skills while looking for permanent positions.

Different Types of Law Firms

When you become a lawyer you can work in a large firm, small firm or go into solo practice. You might want to work in a large firm first for experience and then open your own firm depending on what type of law you are specializing in.

In most firms, lawyers are hired as associates. This is an entry-level position and it is a lateral position, which can last for years. It will probably be a salaried position. You will be paired with one or more experienced partners. If you see this pairing as a positive thing you can learn a lot. As a new associate you probably will not have contact with the client. You will most likely be doing research and drawing up documents. As a new associate you will not have control over the cases or the work you do. However, at this early stage of your career, you will not have to worry about the business side of the firm such as bringing in new clients. In a small firm you will most likely deal with clients and take on significant responsibilities early in your career. You will probably work with other lawyers in informal mentoring conferences. In small firms lawyers are often not specialized, you may have to practice many different types of law.

As a solo lawyer or if you work with one or two other lawyers you will have to worry about the business side of your firm. You must have the skills of anyone who is running their own business. In addition to knowing your specialized law you will have to bring in new clients with advertising, networking and marketing. Also in running your own business you have to put in the hours and the work to make it a success. If you want to start your own business it will most likely be easier in a small town or suburban area as long as there is a need for your legal service. In such communities competition from larger established law firms is less. Starting a practice is expensive and risky and should be considered only after you gained some experience.

If you work in a large firm you will also be expected to work very long hours, including holidays. The firm will establish a high number of billable hours that you will have to achieve each year. Even in a smaller firm there may be considerable pressure to produce billable hours and this can affect your personal and family life. Many associates in firms' work long hours for years and never get offered a partnership position.
Most firms have an orientation for new associates. This orientation can range from the red carpet treatment to a causally introduction. On average you can expect your first day to consist of meeting and greeting the people who you will be working with the closest. You will get a tour of the firm so you will know your way around. The firm's overview and polices will be discussed.

Your First Job and the All Important Summer Internship

After deciding what location you wish to live in, what area of law, and what size firm, it is wise to get some experience in this field. During the summers in law school, you must make sure to obtain an internship with a firm, organization or corporations you wish to work for. Many law students obtain their first job from places that they interned with over the summer. Internships are a great way for you to try a firm or organization to see if the job would be something you would truly like to do, while giving the firm or organization an idea of how good an employee you are. A summer internship also looks great on your resume if you later decide to look for other employment opportunities. Competition for these internships can be intense. Make sure you start buffing up your resume early by joining any campus organizations and taking classes on your specific interests. A true passion for an area of law is one of the best ways to make yourself stand out from other candidates.

Almost all law schools have career centers that help you polish your resume, draft cover letters, chose writing samples and find perspective employers that meet your preferences. Many large law firms, organizations and corporations also come with alumni. Although alumni might not have job opportunities available, they are a wealth of knowledge when trying to decide what field is right for you or what type of jobs you should go after.

Conclusion

This chapter has helped you realize the importance of certain factors when seeking a position in law; location, setting, type of law and salary. The high competition for law positions makes it necessary to choose, which of these factors is the most important to you. You probably won't be able to get all your choices in your first position so go for the things that mean the most to you. By reading this chapter you should have been able to narrow down the most important factor you want in a law position.

This chapter gave you the salaries and the different ways a lawyer gets paid. You now know about what you would earn in any position that you seek. It also informed you of the best states for lawyers seeking certain positions, such as New York, California, Texas, Florida and Illinois.

It explained the three sections of the law, general population, governments' section and the business market and where the opportunities are. It gave you hints on how to market yourself in new areas of law such as computer law or in local business affairs.

The willingness to relocate may be the advantage in getting a job or particular type of law you decide to specialize in and if you have some advanced skill in that area, it may help you get a position in that specialty. What type of setting do you want to work in will also determine finding a position. How do you want to earn your money, salaried, billable hours or contingencies? If you want a salaried staff position in a large or government firm you will have a better chance of getting a position if you are in the areas that have these types of firms. If you want to start your own business it will most likely be easier in a small town or suburban area as long as there is a need for your type of legal service. You will probably hold five to eight positions in the forty years between law school and retirement and also make at least one major change in your career.

For getting your first job, it is important to obtain summer internships and to use your schools career center for information on potential employers, career fairs and alumni.

This chapter enlightened you on the important factors in finding a position in law. You should now have determined which factor is most important to you. Now you have a better concept of where and what types of a position to seek. Be versatile and open minded when seeking your first position and you will land that first all-important best position for you.

"For anyone contemplating becoming a Lawyer..."

So You Want To Be A
Lawyer?

Official
Know-It-All
Guide

Marianne Pilgrim Calabrese
Susanne Mary Calabrese

Chapter Seven

Partners and Colleagues

For most people, the perfect working conditions would be a law firm focused on business with the benefits of a professional environment and a friendly atmosphere. It would be nice if the lawyers worked on individual projects by conferring with each other. This rapport between attorneys would give the best possible legal service to the clients and also make the job rewarding. The structures in the legal profession, however, do not necessarily foster this type of atmosphere.

If you work in a large firm you will find there is a hierarchical structure. The hierarchical structure that will affect your day to day life looks something like this:

Management Committee
Equity Partners
Managing Partner/Administrator
Partners
Junior Partners
Of counsel
Senior Associates
Junior Associates,
Summer Associates
Staff Attorneys
Paralegal or Legal Secretaries
Secretaries/Clerks

A management committee most often controls the partnership, although in many patriarchal firms a managing partner retains many powers. In some law firms the administrator assumes many of the responsibilities of the managing partner.

Whatever type of firm you work for, you must remember that partners, especially equity partners who hold a stake in the profit of the firm, are the most important people in the building. They have the most power to make changes and decisions about how the firm is run. There is a simple reason for this – they are the ones who bring in the business and make the money. The cases and clients that a partner manages are what generates the work needed to keep everyone else's job necessary. Money and quantity of clients is the number one deciding factor when it comes to power in the office.

Some partners are wonderful people who are very self-sufficient, friendly and approachable. Some are not. As in any career, this varies with the individual. For example, some partners do not wish to complete daily activities such as using their computer or coffee machine and leave these tasks to their secretaries or other support staff. In the extreme, there have been partners who are so reliant on others that they place their pencils in their outboxes to be sharpened. These are obviously not the majority, but when you do come across them, and you will, it is best to try to avoid direct contact   This is not true in just the career in law but these people are found in all professions. As a junior associate, they are the ones who are most likely to talk down to you, give you mundane work with little instruction and be the least understanding. Working directly with their secretary or paralegal is usually the easiest and most efficient way of completing your case assignments. These are the things no one wants to tell you but they do go on in a law firm and you will have to learn to deal with them to survive.

On the other hand, some partners are incredibly understanding of junior associates and explain assignments thoroughly. Usually these are the attorneys who are self-sufficient in office procedures. Regardless of the type of client or case you are working on, assignments with these type of partners will be the most rewarding type of work, where you will learn the most.

Because so many associates are coming up for partner, many offices are adapting a hierarchy system within their partners as well. Those partners who generate the most business for the firm and have paid money toward the firm have an equal share in the firm's profits. Some junior partners who have less clients can also be conferred the title of partner and be able to make management decisions, yet not be given a share in the firm's profits.

Of Counsel are attorneys that the firm employees for their expertise in a certain area of law. These are senior attorneys who are not partners, but have a formal relationship with the firm. For example, the term may be used for a senior partner of a law firm who has gone into semi-retirement or a lateral hire who may be in line for partnership after a prescribed amount of time with the firm. Of Counsel who is semi-retired, are usually very knowledgeable and usually work fewer hours than those of a partner. For this reason, these people are sometimes easier to approach with questions than partners because they have more time and patience to explain answers. It is quite beneficial to become friendly with someone in this category, not only for their legal expertise, but because they most likely have long term relationships with many of the firm partners, have wonderful tricks-of-the-trade and amusing legal stories that they are often willing to pass along. They are usually just great people to know.

The majority of the other attorneys in a law firm or even in a corporation are associates. Senior associates are probably the busiest and most stressed attorneys in the office. They are attorneys who have been practicing law for 6-8 years and will shortly be considered for partner. Many of these attorneys have their own clients or matters that they handle exclusively. Unfortunately, even the most skilled attorney will have trouble advancing to the position of partner if they do not manage clients of their own. Often a junior associate, one who is shortly out of law school, will assist a senior associate in a case.

These junior associates are salaried lawyers in the firm who, depending on the firm, are trained by more experienced lawyers in a specific area of practice. Junior positions provide opportunities for instruction, the highest initial starting salaries, a sense of security, and a chance to practice law with other attorneys who are generally able to provide the benefit of valuable experience. However working for a big law firm as an associate you may find you don't have the freedom of hours you work or the kinds of clients you have. Partners have earned the freedom to work when they want to, but associates must complete the assignments that a partner gives them and bill as many hours as possible.

Staff Attorneys are also a possible type of employment at a law firm. They are attorneys who are hired on a temporary basis in order to complete a work intensive case. Often these attorneys are hired to go through boxes of documents or organize major document productions. Many of these attorneys hope to gain permanent employment at the firm once the case they are assigned to is complete. These attorneys are very eager to please and usually work very hard and long hours, hoping to prove themselves to the firm.

Summer Associates are law students who have completed their first or second year of law school and who work the summer at the firm. These summer associates are paid perspective candidates for jobs with the firm as soon as they graduate law school, and most receive offers from the firm. As a summer associate, the firm instructs you on different areas of practice, throws outings and events in order for you to meet and form relationships with the other, more senior, attorneys and gives you case assignments that would be expected of a junior associate.

It is highly recommended that you obtain a summer associate position while in law school to expand your knowledge of how a firm works and to increase your chances of finding employment after graduation. As a summer associate, you also build lasting relationships with attorneys who can help you in the future. In corporations, these summer positions are called internships and in many cases they also lead to permanent employment upon graduation.

Whether there is a legal staff, or an individual full time lawyer employed by the corporation the chief legal officer in a corporation is usually referred to as the general counsel. The general counsel reports to the president or Chief Executive Officer of the corporation. In addition to a general counsel, corporations have associate general counsels corresponding to partners in a law firm in terms of experience and assistant general counsels corresponding to associates. Both law firms and general corporations use the committee system to spread out policy decisions and work. These committees may or may not include associates.

As a new lawyer you will fall into the category of associates. These are salaried lawyers in the firm who, depending on the firm, can expect to be considered for partnership after six to eight years.

Paralegal and Legal Secretaries

A paralegal or legal secretary can gather research information and in many other ways pull facts for a case. Generally a paralegal is given duties in reaching library and government records for past legal decisions that affect the case. Research is the main component in the paralegal's work.

A legal secretary 's duties include correspondence, at the direction of the legal assistant/paralegal or attorney. They also are responsible for court documents being filed properly, on time, and in the right court. They are responsible for the legal office work.

As a new associate you can learn a lot from an experienced paralegal or legal secretary. They can get the word out very quickly about the new associate. So treat them with respect and you will be rewarded.

The Associate's Role in the Social Order

Being an associate is being smack in the middle of the social order of a firm and sometimes they are on the bottom being the most dispensable members of the firm. As an associate you are subject to demands from members above you, such as the senior associates, of counsel, junior partners, partners and especially equity partners and responsibly for paralegal and legal secretaries below you.

Social acceptance is something needed to work in a firm. You must strive to be socially accepted especially by the partners. You may be great at you job but you need to be accepted by the partners, they have to feel they can work with you. However discontented you might be with the social system you must follow certain rules to survive in the system. Some of the rules are:

1. Always agree with the partners, especially with the equity partners. If you must disagree, do it very limitedly and respectfully.
2. Don't criticize a colleague at a meeting
3. Don't complain about paralegal or legal secretaries to co-workers

4. Talk to an associate or paralegal or secretary privately about a problem
5. Choose your clique of associates or partners and socialize with them.
6. Don't try to change the procedures of the firm or department.
7. Don't do any part of another associates job unless the partner in charge asks you to.
8. Don't complain to a partner about another associate.
9. Learn the best way to communicate with the equity partners.
10. Work with the best paralegal or legal secretary for you.
11. Make a support group that you feel comfortable with and can go to for information and advise.

New associates who do not obey these rules to some degree will be looked upon as a potential radical or troublemaker. As a new associate you must focus on your strengths and weaknesses in relation to the social rules of your firm, as well as identifying your friends and foes before you can ease into a firm. Associates require many interactions with partners, other associates, paralegals, legal secretaries, and clients: each type of interaction is different. An associate should be in a leadership position when working with paralegals and legal secretaries and in the role of equal when working with fellow new associates and the role of subordinate when interacting with partners. You can be all of these roles to some degree when working with clients. The varieties of an associate's social interaction all require different interpersonal skills, thus making any affiliation complex.

Don't get caught between two partners with different views. Be smart, say nothing about which view you think is best. Let the partners figure it out. Just state the facts about the case. If you say something in either direction you might offend one of the partners. You do not want to do that. If they don't outwardly ask your opinion, don't give it. Don't volunteer your opinion especially if it may alienate one of the partners.

Partner's Favorites

The easiest way to become a favorite is to know someone, preferable an equity partner in the firm. You should try all your connections while looking for a position and if you land a position where you know people you are ahead of the game. If however you find yourself in a firm where you do not know anyone, you will have to do a little work socializing in order to gain a popular spot.

First if you do a good job, bill many hours and bring in clients of your own that will very quickly bring you respect. If you can't get more clients and bring in more money than the average associate in your firm than find a support group and try to break into the clicks of partners.

Building a Support System

You will need a support group in order to survive in a large law firm. How do you perceive support? Do you give support as well as accept it? Where will you get your support from, will it come from other associates or from partners or maybe even from paralegals or secretaries? Here are some questions that will help you find and interact with the right support group. Answer each question with the name of a person you would most likely go to. If you would solve it yourself, write no one.

1. When on a case and you have a question who would you go to for the answer?
2. If you have a client that was particularly troublesome, whom would you go to?
3. If you had a bad day and wanted to talk, whom would you go to?
4. If your were finding it hard to work with one of the partners, whom would you go to?
5. If you wanted to know the latest gossip in the office, whom would you go?
6. If you wanted to find out more about a client, whom would you go to?
7. If you thought a group of associates were treating you badly, to whom would you go to?
8. If you were angry with another associate, to whom would you go to?
9. If you thought a case was not being handled properly by a senior partner, to whom would you go to?

10. If you were able to help a client in a special way, to whom would you go to?
11. If one of your cases did unusually well, to whom would you go to?
12. If a senior partner gave you a compliment on your work with a particular case, to whom would you go to?
13. If you found a new and better way of doing a procedure, to whom would you go to?

Check your answers. Do you have a lot of "No One" answers? If you have more 'no ones' than names then you might want to think about adding more people to your support system. Remember that everyone needs other people, because you can't do everything by yourself. Also, do you use one person's name frequently? If so, you may be depending on one person too much. Are you reciprocating? Remember that you are part of other people's support systems. This may be the start of a friendship or the group you will fit in with, so set up some time to nurture the relationships with the people with whom you feel comfortable.

Work Friends

When making friends at work, you must be careful. There are friends and then there are friends from work. It is possible to make a true friend at work but if a person has to choose between a friendship formed at work or the job itself, nine times out of ten he will pick the job. People are there for the job, especially if they have student loans, mortgages, rent, and kids in college, etc. Most people want to be friendly, but when push comes to shove, a job is wanted more than a friendship in most cases. If all of a sudden the main equity partner didn't like you, and you'll be out of a job soon, you will be shocked at how fast most of your work friends will treat you as if you had the plague. They would be afraid to be around you because they might become associated with you and also lose their jobs. I know this is a little disheartening, but it is a reality in the legal profession and no one wants to tell you this.

Associate Interactions

Co- associates are important in meeting your social and support needs: they are the primary source of advice and support. However you are all in competition for partnerships and even though you are in the same boat there is competition. So keep this in mind and take this into consideration when working with them. Most associates both initiate and welcome exchange of ideas and sociability but it would also be a good idea to make social and professional contact with the partners in the firm.

Evaluation

You are constantly being evaluated in the firm. First, if you socialize with the partners and have a good rapport with them you will have a good chance of getting a good evaluation. Second, if your firm has the policy of billable hours you must have reached or exceeded your billing goals. The partners and their clients, who you have worked with must be satisfied with you

Tier System

The traditional pyramid structure of the law firm is thick at the bottom with new associates and narrow at the top with partners. Changes in the way time is billed is slowly changing the pyramid to a diamond structure, which is thick in the middle with experienced lawyers and other revenue-generating producers and thin on support staff and management. The tier system still exists in most firms. However some law firms have changed hiring criteria to more aptly fit the required skill set. All departments provide upward mobility to lawyers; although mobility is not as rapid as in other industries, often associates move up according more to years of service and amount of clients held, rather than legal merit. The tier system, though, allows the partnership to regulate a fairly legitimate and objectively applied system. Firms are starting to hire fewer associates and their chances of making partner are far lower than they once were. A tiered system can have the following titled positions: Staff Attorney, Junior Associate, Senior Associate, Equity Partner, Managing Partner, and Of Counsel.

Generation Gap

There are generally two types of generations working today, the older baby boomers and the new younger Generation X. When you get in a law firm you are going to have to learn to work with both no matter which group you fall into.

If you are a young Generation X lawyer you may have watched your parents become victims of Corporate America, they were laid off, downsized or merged into oblivion. They were loyal to the firm and expected to be employed there until retirement. You did not learn about loyalty to the law firm or corporation, instead you might have learned to make your own breaks. Your computer skills are probably second language to you and you are more prone to take charge of your own career.

If you are a baby boomer you lived with the free spirit of the 60's and have been in the work place for awhile. You are a descended of longevity and loyalty to the firm and you hadn't learned about a computer until college. You feel the firm will take care of you and your career until you retire.

Whether you are new Generation X or a baby boomer you can learn from each other and you have to learn to work with each other. First listen to what the other has to say. There has never been a time when there has been such a wonderful combination of talent and expertise. Maximize, maneuver and manage it. Here are some guidelines that will help you collaborate with each other.

1. Baby boomers must listen to the new Generation X when it comes to computers. They may be more computer literate then you. New Generation X lawyers should beware, the baby boomer may have written the software you are using in your computer

2. Baby boomers, you depend on your job to teach you what you need. Don't get offended if the new Generation X tackles the job scene differently than you. The new Generation X is wary about depending on employers for the assets they will need to build successful careers, so they create their own breaks.

3. Boomers you are used to the hierarchical pyramid, the new Generation X expects the manager to be hands on and to work

for his or her subordinates.

4. Boomers, when training new Generations X don't expect them to learn in a step by step way. They were brought up on high tech simulations.

5. The motto work hard, be loyal, move up may be replaced by work harder to make up for lost colleagues, expect little in return.

The Challenges of Billing Hours

Some law positions require billable hours. The major difference between working in the field of law and working in any other salaried position is that you have to bill your hours. In all actuality, being a lawyer is doing contract work all the time. Every hour that you work has to be billed to a client at an hourly rate determined by the firm, and the revenue generated from your billed hours is what turns a profit. Make no mistake about it, you must bill lots and lots of hours to be successful at your job, and in some instances, even keep your job. Each firm expects an employee to bill a certain number of hours over the year. At the end of the year, if an individual bills more than the required amount of hours, they may earn a bonus with the amount contingent upon how many excess hours were billed.

It may sound like a huge burden to write down what you did for clients during each and every minute of your day, but this must be done. Billing time is a double-edged sword. Because attorneys are essentially contractors, it doesn't matter when they actually bill this time, so long as the work is finished. Regardless of your schedule, if you have to bill 2000 hours in a year you cannot take off large amounts of time – and face time is expected in most firms.

Many attorneys are able to work whatever hours they like, coming into the office very late or very early depending on their preference or merely to work at home. Lawyers also have the ability to leave in the middle of the day for hours at a time to do whatever they please (long lunches, home delivery, shopping, etc.) and then return later, or simply work more hours another time in the week. In corporations there is some work time flexibility but you will always be required to be there during the core hours of the day.

So if working in a firm is so flexible, why do so many attorneys become burnt out and stressed? Attorneys often do not take advantage of the opportunities they have. When work is slow, like during the summer or during holiday times, many lawyers remain in the office but are unable to bill time to a client. During this time, you, as an associate should make the most of the free time you are given. Time that you are not billing is your own time, not the firms. Money talks – the firm does not care what you do with your time, unless you are billing hours. It is obviously important to make a good impression on your partners and senior associates, but make sure you balance your home life with the flexible time law firm attorneys are given.

Life as an attorney requires time management that is different from that of other salaried jobs. Taking a long lunch with loved ones now and then or going shopping with friends when you are not busy is incredibly important to building a balanced life. This will seriously decrease the chances that you will become one of those ashen-faced, burnt-out attorneys when the time comes when many hours are needed to complete a particular case matter or filing. Having to work 80-hour weeks at one point during the year won't feel quite as bad if the month before you used your time wisely for your personal matters. Both billable hour and salaried positions have this problem.

Unsupervised, Supervised and Supervisory Work Categories

Lawyers' work falls into three categories, unsupervised, supervised and supervisory. As a lawyer you will probably work in all three categories during your career.

Unsupervised lawyers work with their client alone. There is a one on one client lawyer relationship. The lawyer personally handles the client's work, offers advice, and represents the client's goals.

Supervised lawyers work under a senior lawyer. They don't normally have direct contact with the client. Sometimes the law firm itself will represent the clients. This exists in more complex cases where the lawyers are both supervisors and supervised. This arrangement is common in corporate law departments. In all cases the lawyers at the top are in charge of the representation and responsible directly to the client.

Supervisory lawyers may handle parts of the client's case alone and may have some of the clients work delegated to other attorneys or be supervised by other attorneys. Some supervision is required in all but the simplest routine legal work. The supervisor also works with non-legal support staff.

Mostly, the experienced attorneys do supervisory and unsupervised work while the less experienced are supervised. New lawyers who do unsupervised work are the ones starting their own practice. They may not have the benefit of senior lawyers to help them.

In most positions you begin with supervised work and then move on to unsupervised and then graduate to supervisory positions. But don't be surprised if you find yourself, first day on a job, in a district attorney's office with a pile of files on your desk and an appointment to be in court at 10:00 AM that morning. This is not uncommon. It is also not uncommon for an experienced lawyer to work in a supervised situation, particularly on a complicated case.

Conclusion

In this chapter you were introduced to the higher structure of most large law firms, the working arrangement, how to recognize the pecking order and ways to succeed in it. It explained the power of the partners and how they can effect your position. You learned that equity partners, who hold a stake in the profits, are the most important people in the office. They have the most power over your success or failure. So learn how to please them.

You now know that as an associate you do not have the same liberties as a partner. You will have to complete assignments that a partner gives you and bill as many hours as possible. Now you have more insight into the generation gap. No matter if you are a boomer or a new Generation X you now know the importance of interacting and working successfully with each other.

This chapter explained how to regulate you time in order to become more efficient socially as well as professionally. It also gave you hints on how to avoid burnout from working long hours. It gave you a clear understanding of unsupervised, supervisory and supervised work and how and when to expect to work under each condition.

This chapter gave you key ideas such as getting sociable with key people in the firm and understanding how to make your goals known. Work within the hierarchical environment of the firm in order to achieve your plans and goals. Make sure you learn and respect the people at the top of the ladder. Find a comfortable level of interaction within the social structure. The most important factor is pleasing the partners, especially the equity partners. Being an associate is being smack in the middle of the social order. The rules, hints, and procedures outlined in this chapter will help you with these social order relationships and you will find you can ease into a law firm.

"For anyone contemplating becoming a Lawyer..."

So You Want To Be A
Lawyer?

Official Know-it-All Guide

Marianne Pilgrim Calabrese
Susanne Mary Calabrese

Chapter Eight

How to Deal with Clients, Colleagues and Paralegals

A Client's Poem

If Only You'd Ask, I'd Be Happy To Say…

If only you'd ask, I'd be happy to say
I wish you would do things more often my way

If only you'd ask, I'd be happy to say
I'd don't like that new partner that calls everyday

If only you'd ask, I'd be happy to say
I'd like you to bill me in an alternative way

If only you'd ask, I'd be happy to say
We have four new matters that came in just today

If only you'd ask, I'd be happy to say
Being responsive to me means you call back the same day

If only you'd ask, I'd be happy to say
There are three other law firms we're considering today

If only you'd ask, I'd be happy to say
I expect your budget to reflect what I'll pay

If only you'd ask, I'd be happy to say
When you go over budget, I see my career slip away

If only you'd ask, I'd be happy to say
I wish you would do things more often my way

By Felice Wagner

You want to learn to deal with clients, colleagues and paralegals in ways that will ensure your success. You do not want to experience verbal lashing or worse, from a vindictive colleague, administrator or even the firms' best client. There are ways that will ensure your success and enable you to interact with clients, colleagues and paralegal successfully. It is important to keep emotional stress down to its lowest level. Emotional abuse can run rampant in a workplace especially in a law firm. The great American workplace secret is that emotional abuse is more prevalent than sexual, age or race discrimination. This chapter will give you hints on how to relate successfully with clients, colleagues and paralegals.

Clients

Lawyers or law firms perform work in collaboration with the client for the benefit of the client. The relationship is contractual, the client has some goal such as forming a corporation, filing a lawsuit or getting a divorce, etc. A client's relationship to the lawyer is different than an employee who works under the client. The lawyer is entrusted to make certain decisions about the client's case. The client controls the objectives of the goals and the lawyer controls the way the case is handled to achieve the goals.

The ideal relationship you can have with the client is to be his advocate and at the same time feel that justice is being done. Conflicts can arise between your responsibilities to the clients and the legal system and with your own interests in remaining an upright person while earning a satisfactory living. The Rules of Professional Conduct prescribe terms for resolving some conflicts. Many such issues can be resolved through sensitive professional and moral judgment.

There is major competition for clients. You can not sit back and expect clients to appear; you have to go out and recruit them and then keep them satisfied. Competition has forced firms to give quality service and lower fees. Some firms fall into the trap of getting too involved in the technical side of law and neglect the people side. Even though law firms do advertising, the best way of acquiring clients still remains referrals. No one wants to refer a lawyer or firm where he has been poorly treated.

Clients want to be treated fairly. Economics has forced clients to become active; they want to do business with firms that not only produce the best work but also have the best service at the lowest fees. Lawyers have learned to acknowledge this for survival.

Components to Good Client Relations

There are basically two components to good client relations, technological and personal. The technical component consists of the procedures used to deliver the legal services in the case, while the personal side is the verbal interaction between you and the client.

Some tips to have the technical side run smoothly are:

- Explain the case to your support team.
- Have backup support people and know how to get in touch with them at all times.
- Always know the status of the case and let your team know this information.
- Give clear assignments and deadlines.
- Know how much the case will cost and who and how to charge.

Some tips for the personal side are:

- The initial interview is one of the most important things, it is your time to decide if you can and want to handle the case.
- After you have agreed to accept representation schedule a conference with you and the client to bond.
- Explain fully your policy as to fees.
- Always respond to telephone calls from the client.
- Always inform the client of communication, written or oral from your adversary.
- Every offer and counterproposal should be reviewed with

the client.
- Never give the client the impression you are too preoccupied with other matters to devote whatever attention is necessary to his or her particular matter. A large percentage of your success with a client has to do with the confidence and empathy you are able to instill.
- Always do you homework before seeing a client; never give the impression that you have forgotten details previously furnished.
- When the case is completed express you appreciation to the client.

In general, always have someone on your support team available to talk to the client if you are not available. Have personnel know the client's name and something about their case. Try to be compassionate especially on cases that are emotional, for example divorce cases. Also, remember to be courteous to your clients. Don't call meetings that will not result in a decision. Keep deadline promises made to the client. Make sure the client's bill is prepared properly. Always go the extra mile and ask the client if you can meet them in their office so you can meet all the members of their team, if appropriate. If the client gets a little nasty don't respond likewise back. Keep in mind this is more of an emotional experience for him. Don't over promise or under deliver. The general rule of thumb is to make clients feel important - the more important they feel the better they will feel about using you.

Relationships with Clients

How involved you get with your clients is up to how comfortable both you and your client feel. There are, however some guidelines that you should always professionally follow. Having dinner with clients, treating them with sports tickets or small gifts of appreciation is always a good idea, as long as it is tactfully done. All people like to feel they are getting something extra and that their business is important to you. However, never let personal feelings get out of hand. For example, developing a romantic relationship with a client is very dangerous to your career. Sexual relationships with clients are a very sensitive problem. States such as California and New York have passed regulations prohibition sexual relationships with clients. Certainly, sex between consenting adults is accepted but the problem in relationships between lawyers and their clients, particularly in divorce cases, could be construed as unethical because there is a conflict of interest. Try not to get involved with your clients. It will put your job and your credibility at risk.

Types of Clients

There are, as many types of clients as there are people but you will find the type of cases will make the type of client. Clients are the most emotional in domestic litigation, divorces, child custody, separations, adoptions, or any time you are dealing with someone's family. Murder cases are not as emotional, because these people are usually more torn up than the murder victim's family. In General, it is very hard to deal with people who are thinking with their emotions but they don't realize it. They are so hurt they can't think straight. Even if they win their case, they don't feel any better because the legal win doesn't heal the emotional scar. That comes as a shock to them.

If you get a car accident case the client comes in, you get the medical report, take the deposition and maybe have two meetings. But with domestic litigation clients, they will interact with you almost every week because they are so upset. Particularly if they have children, they must always cope with the visitations and exchanges and will pass their anxiety onto you.

Image Is Important

Because clients do not have a degree in law, (which is precisely why they hired you) it is difficult for them to perceive how you are doing throughout a case. Especially in litigation matters where the stakes for the client are high, it is important to put your best face forward. This means that simple things like preparing professional looking binders with labels and tabs and organizing their materials efficiently have an incredibly beneficial effect on client relations.

For example, there was one case where two co-defendants each had separate attorneys. One attorney was perfectly familiar with all the materials and had great legal skills, but appeared quite disorganized. The other attorney also did a good job representing his client, but had made up a series of binders that were beautifully labeled and organized. Something as simple as a professional looking organizational system made all the difference. Throughout the trial and even after, the client raved about the quality of the attorney's work. The attorney did, in fact, have legal skill, but no more than the other attorney who did not put his best foot forward.

Make sure the client sees that you have a good grasp of his case, that you are giving it the proper attention, and always appear professional and organized. This type of organization is also effective when writing up business proposals and meeting with new clients. It is the first impression and your appearance of professionalism that makes the most difference. It is the small touches, such as using professional binder labels and tabs, something that your legal secretary can do for you in a matter of minutes that can change the way a client perceives you.

Never Underestimate Who the Client Is

Often in big firms, there will be enormous cases for which a dozen or so people will be dedicated to full time. These cases usually have rooms filled with boxes of materials and documents pertinent to the case. These cases usually involve specific companies and attorneys from a private firm. They will often have to work with the in-house counsel of these companies. Sometimes attorneys will have to work at a company office for weeks at a time collecting documents or testimony related to a particular case. Sometimes, attorneys may have to work in-house even longer.

Always remember who your client is when working outside the firm. When you work with in-house counsel, it is easy to mistake them for one of your team and to forget that, although they are working as attorneys for a company, they are also your clients. These attorneys pay the bill and are whom you are working for on a case.

A group of attorneys were working at a company reviewing documents with members of the company's in-house counsel. After several weeks of working at the company, one of the attorneys made an off-handed comment about how the case was being treated to a member of the in-house counsel. The member of the in-house counsel, in turn, repeated the comment to a senior attorney. As the comment spread, it greatly decreased the amount of respect the company had for the firm it hired. Because these issues got in the way of the firm and the company working together, the case and future business relations greatly suffered. Avoid this situation in your own career and keep negative comments to yourself.

Know Your Assignment

A young single attorney, Mary, worked for a large law firm in New York City. The firm was working on an important case in Chicago. There came a time in the fall that a group of attorneys, including Mary, were asked to go and spend about six weeks at the client's site to do research, pertaining to the case. They would be put in a hotel, be given generous food allowances and be flown home every weekend if they desired. Well Mary knew she had to go because this would be a good opportunity for her to advance her career. Besides it was only for six to eight weeks. She gave up most of her personal life in New York and went to Chicago. She was treated very well there. She was put in a beautiful hotel, ate in the finest restaurants and flew wherever she wanted on weekends. By the following spring the entire group was still in Chicago Mary became very burned out and longed for the case to be over. She asked to be transferred back to New York but was told that only when the case was completed would she be transferred back. She wound up quitting and going back to New York to be with her family and friends.

Make sure you can handle long stays away from home. Realize that six to eight weeks' relocation for a case can mean a lot longer. No one is going to tell you this when you get into a law firm. Relocation with all the generous amenities sounds very appealing, but you may get more than you bargained for. So think long and hard before you accept temporary relocation to work on a case. It is easier to initially decline than to try to return before the case is closed.

On the other hand, if you are seriously dedicated to your field of practice and do not mind giving up your life for months at a time, then working on a long-term assignment might be an excellent way to set yourself apart from others in the firm. Not only will you likely be given much responsibility and meet important people, your commitment shows you are a dedicated attorney who is willing to make sacrifices for the firm.

Billing Practices for Clients

Another great tip when working with clients is to remember to be well aware of the billing practices employed by your firm. For example, there have been horror stories of some clients being completely satisfied with an attorney's work, but were unwilling to pay for the services required. Your firm requires you to bill any time worked on a client's case and billing for this time is how your firm makes money. However, some clients will complain when they are billed for file organization, telephone conversations or other forms of advice. Make sure you know what the client will pay for and structure your billing of time accordingly. It will save you and your client a lot of time, not to mention ill-will, if you do not have to fight over every minute the client will not pay for because you were not aware of the correct billing practices.

Colleagues

As a new attorney you will have to learn and work with the politics of the office. Most offices will be in the realm of normality and you will be able to ease into it. There will be, on rare occasion, where an experienced lawyer might be extra difficult to work with. This is not the occasional flare up or venting of emotions, it is the routine verbal battering by a firm member causing a chaotic environment and anxiety. The management usually tolerates their behavior because they hold an important position, like equitable partner. Rarely is this behavior tolerated from someone who has no strong political or economic standing in the firm. The important lawyers who exhibit this behavior are usually excused or given slaps on the wrist or just labeled difficult to work with. You will have to learn how to handle them.

You will be able to recognize when a firm tolerates the extra difficult lawyer because instead of directly handling the person they will divert to other measures. They may move the lawyer to an office out of the mainstream, or they may tell you that its just the way he is or he is just hard to work with. The difficult attorney may have constant turnovers of work mates such as secretaries. You may hear the management tell him he should not have yelled at an associate in the hallway to do it in his office instead. Or you learn an administrator silently comforted an upset employee in hopes that the partners will talk to the offender. Employees hesitate to answer any messages from him. These are some signs to look for to identify a difficult lawyer. Learn from other employees' mistakes and follow your instincts when you see signs that this attorney is difficult to work with.

Looks can be Deceiving

Some good advice when dealing with other attorneys is that you can never judge the intelligence or importance of a lawyer on first glance. It is important never to underestimate people. At one law firm there was a partner who had terrible hygiene and eating habits. He did not cut his fingernails often enough and had a terrible habit of spitting when he talked. Once when he was out at a client dinner, he ordered a T bone steak, and proceeded to pick up the bone and suck the meat off with his teeth. Basically, on the outside, the man seemed to be a disorganized mess. In actuality, he was a brilliant and well-respected attorney. He just was a little uneducated in social graces, but focused well on his job. When people made the mistake of underestimating his legal talent, there were usually grave consequences. Don't make the same mistake with other attorneys of his type. When working with them, or against them, never underestimate their legal cunning or importance in the firm.

Your Competition

As a junior associate, beware of those associates that are only a year or two more your senior. The profession of law attracts many people who like to be in charge and enjoy delegating responsibility to others. There was one junior attorney that no other person wanted to work with. She was very demanding of the others and was difficult to work with, preferring to tell others what to do instead of doing the work herself. There was one occasion where she was assigned to work on a case with another attorney who was only a year junior to her at the firm. This junior attorney had gotten the flu and came in the office briefly to speak with the partner she worked with. After he had told her to go home to get some rest, this attorney came into her office and demanded that she finish some research for her. She refused to let her go home, even when she learned that the partner had sent her home. She preferred to have this junior attorney do the research for her, although she could have easily done it herself, or waited a few days for the assignment.

Unfortunately, you have to learn to work with these type people or avoid them. You must be careful to sustain good relationships with you colleagues and avoid this behavior. This particular attorney got the reputation of blaming others for her mistakes, of not doing her own work, of being completely dependant on others and had a difficult time throughout the firm finding people willing to help or work with her.

Steps for Interacting Successfully with Clients and Colleagues

There are certain steps you can take to ensure success when working with clients and coworkers. The way you interact and respond to them will ensure your success. You have control over how you respond and react so you have power over the situation to a certain extent.

How you portray yourself has an overall effect on your success. Portray yourself as a positive, confident, easygoing professional, even if you are not. If you appear nervous, angry, emotionally upset, hostile, or negative in any way, your chances of succeeding can decrease.

In situations of conflict, how you carry yourself is particularly important Especially with co-workers, first try to listen for the facts without getting emotional. It is hard, but try to not take it personally. Skillful listening and feedback techniques will help you find the real problem. Your body posture, tone of voice and facial expression can all affect this. Look the person straight on, at appropriate times stop talking and remain calm. Concentrate on what the person is trying to say. Add to the conversation things like: "If I understood you correctly you want…"

When a person is upset they need to make their point understood, save face, feel important and get satisfaction. You have to try to acknowledge these emotions neutrally by letting them know you are trying to understand or that you do understand. Apologize if you think it is warranted or if not try to compromise by using neutral statements such as: "I'm sorry this happened, " I'm sorry you are upset with my assignment results." Or "I understand how you have reached that conclusion. However, let me present a different interpretation of the data." If you want to reach an agreement try statements like: "What is the next step?" " What do you think is a fair way to settle this?" Or "Let me give you a different perspective on that." Ultimatums are not a good idea; they usually are not effective.

Try to avoid putting yourself in a situation where you will be in danger. Always be in tune to nonverbal communications, clenched fists, tensed body, or red-faced body language that makes you uncomfortable. At this point you can excuse yourself professionally and politely and say: "I'll just be a moment" or "I have to look up something, I'll be right back." This will give everyone a time out and you will have time to decide what to do next.

The Firm's Policy

You can try to make it the firm's responsibility to handle abusive behavior. If you have been with the firm for awhile and feel you can get enough co-worker and especially partner support, you may try to put some firm policy in effect. Don't do this unless you can get enough key co-worker support. You don't want to be labeled the one who is doing this alone. Don't put your job in jeopardy trying to implement a difficult firm procedure or even change a firm's policy. Make it a group project; it is important to get experienced attorneys involved.

When is it Time to Change a Position?

There will be many reasons why you may want to change your position. Most people don't stay at one firm for their entire careers. You may find you want to move on after a few years. Maybe you want to start your own practice, try a different type of law or go where the other lawyers are more to your liking. No matter where you work, you will want to feel included and recognized, competent and in control, accepted and liked by others, as well as be able to make a living.

The trick is to change positions because you want to fulfill you career goals. Changing a position needs to be well thought out. Some reasons for leaving might be, a better opportunity to meet your goal plans, no more opportunity for improvement or growth at your current firm, your position no longer meets your qualifications, or an opportunity for financial gain. The main thing behind the move should be to define your career goals.

Some questions to ask yourself before leaving are;

1. What is the main reason I want to leave?

2. Can I fix the reason I want to leave, for example by asking for an increase in salary?
3. Do I enjoy my colleagues, support staff etc.?
4. Is my leaving focused on one person or a group? If so who?
5. Is a transfer out of the department possible?
6. Do I enjoy my work?
7. Has the firm changed since I started?
8. Do I like the number of hours I work?
9. What is my definition of job satisfaction?
10. Can I get to where I want to be from here?

Hiring rates are generally best in June and October when firms tend to increase staff. October 15 through January 15 is the slowest hiring period. Corporations have their seasons but generally they are slow around the holidays.

If you do decide to leave your job make sure you have another position before you do so. The new position should fulfill the reasons why you decided to leave your previous position. Never quit your job until your new position is secure. It is also not a good idea to accept a counter offer from your old firm. Make your decision to make a change and then stick to it.

There was an attorney Anna, who decided to leave the law firm where she was working because she was not making enough money. She went on interviews and finally landed a position in an equally prestigious law firm making a desired amount of money. When she gave notice to her firm they counter offered and equaled the salary. Since she liked where she worked, worked well with her colleagues, and didn't particularly like change, she decided to stay. Everything seemed to be fine. She was happy until about six months later when they told her they were downsizing and had to let her go. She was devastated and angry with herself for not leaving when she had the chance. She got the impression the firm felt she wasn't really happy there and when it was time to downsize she was one of the people they felt easy to let go. So don't make the same mistake as Anna. Once you've decided to leave your current law firm and you advise the firm of a new job offer be prepared to leave. If you are not prepared to leave, don't say anything to your present employer, decline the offer and stay with your current firm.

What Legal Secretaries and Paralegals Can Do For You

As a lawyer you will be doing a lot of work preparing for cases. Some of these tasks require your special knowledge of the law, but a paralegal or legal secretary can do others. A paralegal can gather research information and sometimes pull all of the facts of the case together. Besides doing research and paperwork, a paralegal can interact with the client and other people involved in the case.

Generally in a case, paralegals can be given duties in researching library and government records for past legal decisions that affect the case. They also can review law books for laws that support the case, record all the details of the matter, file the appropriate paperwork for the court proceedings, and conduct interviews with clients. They can maintain contact with the client by providing them with updates about the case, which can often be time-consuming for an attorney

Research is the main component in the paralegal work. Assembling and organizing background information and data that will support your case is their primary job. The paralegal has the responsibility of gathering any information relevant to the case. As the information develops, the paralegal gives these findings to the supervising attorney acquires additional assignments or changing the direction of the search. As part of the ongoing process the paralegal organizes and keeps files on the data. They may draft arguments or motion, suggest which witnesses to interview and go into the courtroom to assist you with document management during the trial.When teamed with a lawyer, a paralegal can help with productivity, thus it is extremely cost effective to hire paralegal help. Paralegals often bill their time like attorneys, but at a much lower hourly rate.

The relationship between the client, paralegal and you should be clearly defined. The client must be made aware that the paralegal is acting on your behalf and under your direction and that he/she is not a lawyer. This will save your paralegal the awkward and possibly dangerous situation of being asked for legal advice they are not qualified to give. Although you can also have a paralegal interview possible witnesses, write reports, draft documents, organize files, attend court proceedings and assist you during a trial, it is ultimately your responsibility to handle a case and to apply the appropriate law.

Paralegals are often given office duties too. They can organize employees, maintain the firm's financial files, and organize files on law guidelines and reference materials. Essentially they can be given non-clerical and non-secretarial legal work in assisting you. As with any managerial position, it is a good idea to set boundaries for the paralegals by clearly stating your assignments, but then allow them to operate on their own.

Working with a capable paralegal can be the most beneficial choice you make when starting a law firm. Not only will the efficient use of a paralegal help relieve your workload, but also a paralegal is often privy to the inner workings of the firm. Becoming friendly with a paralegal can often be helpful in learning office policy, gathering office gossip and learning the best ways of doing your tasks. Paralegals can also help you with every sort of random assignment when you are under a strict time crunch or when you have an unusual case. Using paralegals to their full potential is one of the best ways to achieve balance and success in your workplace.

Types of Paralegal Employees

There are two types of paralegal employees, transitional and career. Transitional paralegals usually have graduated from college and are taking a year or two before entering law school or grad school. Their purpose is short term and turnover is encouraged. Firms that tend to hire transitional paralegals sometimes feel that they are getting highly motivated people with superior academic backgrounds.

Career paralegals set out to enter and stay with the field. Educational requirements for career paralegals differ from region to region. Some firms want an "ABA" approved paralegal school graduate. Firms hiring career paralegals tend to feel that they are getting stability, dedication, and the full attention of these employees.

If you work with a somewhat inexperienced paralegal, one who has been working one or two years, you will have to determine which tasks they can perform the best. Most assignments you give should be research or organizational assignments. An experienced paralegal, one with experience of five-years or more, can be given more responsibility. Paralegals can help you take on more cases. The specialized training paralegals receive allows you to practice law, while not getting too bogged down in research organization and paper work. They will save you from having to do a huge amount of time-consuming groundwork.

Duties of Paralegals Working for Corporations, Government ant the Public

A paralegal working for a corporation can be given the responsibility of handling draft agreements, processing Uniform Commercial Code (UCC) searches, directing formation and maintenance of domestic and foreign corporations, participating in bank closings, preparing deeds of trust and real estate documents. Their areas of responsibility and knowledge can include stock insurance, drafting legal agreements, blue-sky laws, and mergers and acquisitions. Securities law, preparing and filing corporate documents, preparing audit letters, assisting with closing commercial bank loans, due diligence on corporate acquisitions regulator and bankruptcy filings can also come within their area of expertise. They should have excellent business writing, drafting, communication, and organizational and interpersonal skills. The ideal ratio of paralegals to attorneys is one paralegal to not more than five attorneys.

The paralegal also can have duties involving the finances of the corporation. Paralegals may work out the details of a loan needed for the business. A corporate maintenance paralegal includes assignments like formation and maintenance of domestic and foreign corporations, partnerships and joint ventures, executing corporate dissolution's and mergers, coordinating domestic qualifications of foreign corporations, preparing closing binders, and drafting corporate resolutions. Maintaining corporate databases, researching the ramifications and consequences of corporate and tax laws may also be assigned to a paralegal. The paralegal must be detail oriented and have excellent follow though skills, while communicating effectively with clients.

Paralegals who work for the public and others in the community may represent a client if it is so authorized by the law. They also are given a great deal of research work in areas such as welfare, social security, medical care, environmental issues, toxic tort, land use, and zoning laws. A paralegal that works in an office of the federal government might be reviewing bankruptcy documents, drafting pleadings such as motions to dismiss or convert cases. Many of the activities, which involved clients, are performed in the presence of an attorney. Many feel that attorneys in private business don't use the paralegal to the full extent. In Response, the federal government has been expanding the role of paralegals.

Litigation Responsibilities

You can expect a paralegal to assist you during litigation. Try to fill litigation paralegal positions with experienced paralegals who have solid litigation support skills. Their duties should include assisting you with documents, preparing depositions, and eventually assisting in the trial preparations. Also they may be involved in determining the needs of the project, selecting litigation support software, selecting hardware, determining what necessary resources will be needed, securing necessary additional office space, interviewing and hiring personnel and overseeing the project to ensure deadlines are met. Trials often require extensive work hours and having a competent paralegal can make this tenuous and stressful time much easier for you.

Giving Assignments to Your Paralegal

There is no program that is right for all firms and legal departments. How the paralegals are used depend on the attitude of the firm. There are many issues that affect the attitude of the firm such as the number of paralegals to attorneys, practice specialties, level of assignments, number of years the firm has employed paralegals, acceptance of clients, billable rates, hiring criteria, job descriptions, turnover rate, profit margin, and other monetary incentives

As a new associate you will have to know how to utilize paralegals from the moment you enter the firm. You may have very different attitudes about paralegals than the senior partners. Any one who has worked in law for more than twenty years probably will not have learned to practice law, while utilizing paralegals. As a new associate you expect paralegals to be part of the practice, the same as computers, secretaries and billable hours. Learn the procedures of the firm. Maybe the assigning of paralegals to attorneys is through a team or a pool. Teams are assigned to certain attorneys and assignments are automatically received only within the team. A pool structure assigns projects according to case or client matters or as a new matter enters the firm. It really comes down to how your associate program is structured. You must conform to the program of your firm.

Whichever system is right for the firm, it is generally more efficient to permanently assign paralegals to the same case or client matter throughout, rather than assign projects on a piecemeal basis. Otherwise background information learned by paralegals and associates become fragmented and no one person knows enough details about the case. Too much time is wasted trying to bring new people up to date.

Paralegals need to know what lawyers want in order to meet their expectations. It is unrealistic to assume any employee will meet and exceed invisible targets and goals. Paralegal programs should be created to keep you happy. If work is not delegated to the paralegal in a competent way, you may get frustrated with the paralegal system. There are two main factors when giving work to paralegals. First is quality of work produced by the paralegal and second their attitude. Can the paralegal get this job done right, on time, correctly, cost effectively, ethically, and efficiently without alienating team members and clients. They must know the steps, listen, and give and execute instructions. Attitude reflects many characteristics, such as motivation and other initiative.

In order to get the most from your paralegal you should know the best ways of working with them. First, don't feel the paralegal is trying to take away your work; market their skills to enhance yours. Having associates perform paralegal work makes little sense. Work should be delegated to persons with the experience, skills, and education to accomplish the project. Here are a few suggestions on how to assign work to a paralegal in order to get the most productivity from them.

Make sure your paralegal is not getting assignments from too many lawyers and cannot prioritize them. Make sure they know how to complete an assignment that you give them. Give the paralegal enough time to complete the assignment, don't routinely give rush deadlines. Be available to assist the paralegal in legal matters in order to complete an assignment. Keep them informed about impending events such as a closing, a deposition, a filing, meeting, etc so that they may anticipate an assignment and complete it on time. If you are working with more than one paralegal, don't just keep one of them informed about the exhibits, factual investigation, status of a document production, etc. You don't want to be in a position of having one person you can only rely on. Give your paralegal asses to online computer services so they can complete assignments. Try to anticipate how much time that the assignment should take to complete and tell the paralegal how long you feel they should have to do it.

Your firm should have some kind of meeting with the paralegals in your firm. Usually meetings are designed according to the number of paralegals. If there is five to fifteen paralegals then a breakfast or lunch meeting might be done once a month. If there is more than fifteen paralegals, the meeting might be divided by practice specialty with only one or two meetings for the entire group each year.

Try to give experienced paralegals more challenging and variety in the work so it doesn't become repetitive and boring. It is common sense that someone will do a better job for you when they enjoy their work.. Tell them what you expect them to do on the assignment. Tell them what they can do, when it has to be delivered, how it has to be delivered and how much time and money you expect it to cost.

You may want to trade billable time for training time. In some instances it might be worth your while to train a paralegal. The advantage to you is you will no longer have to perform paralegal work; a paralegal will be trained to do a certain type of assignment. The client gets a quality work product and saves fees.

In order to do this you first have to negotiate to find out if it would be financially beneficial. Decide how long it would take an experienced paralegal to do an assignment. Say it would take four hours, to train the paralegal, and then the paralegal you want to train will probably take six hours to complete the assignment including two hours of oversight by you. When the assignment is completed, if you approve it, then you can bill the client for four hours and put the other two hours under non-billable time. The paralegal can bill for the six hours that she worked on the assignment at a significantly lower billing rate than yours, saving the client money.

Non-billable time and Write Offs

Sometimes you might want to ask your paralegal to do assignments that are non-billable. The firm may feel these assignments save dollars. Make sure there is a clear understanding about how much non-billable time is allocated. You do not want to give the paralegal too much non-billable time, causing them to complain that it renders them non-profitable to the firm. If the non-billable time serves the firm directly, such as acting as the custodian of records then you may be able to justify the non-billable hours. Get a clear understanding of expectations of this issue. Talk to your fellow lawyers and find out the correct procedure.

The write off for paralegals should be relatively the same as the write off percentage for associates. Although paralegals do very different work than associates, the level of competency applicable to some particular work should be relatively the same. You should know how much time is written off so you know if the write off occurred because of poor work productivity or excessive hours billed.

Your firm may have a pro rata policy. If you want to write off 10 percent of the bill you must cut time from the partner, associate and the paralegal. When cutting only from the bottom, the paralegal is the easiest method but also might be unfair. See what your firm's policy is when using this method.

Never let the paralegal under bill, have them account for all their time. You must understand paralegal profitability to understand the firm's expectations, know the limits of non-billable time and understand the "minimum billable requirements" and allocate time accordingly for your paralegal. Although partners are usually the ones responsible for billing, and understanding of billing practices is essential for all people entering the legal field.

Backup Paralegal Plan

A backup paralegal plan will help you handle unanticipated heavy workloads. When assigning a case give it to a lead paralegal and also a backup paralegal. Inform the backup paralegal of the history of the case, where the documents are, computer/ software system, significant dates etc. It should be the lead paralegal's responsibility to keep the backup paralegal informed. The backup paralegal should be able to step in at a moment's notice to assist when the workload gets heavy.

How to Evaluate Your Paralegal

You will at some point be asked to evaluate the paralegal you have been working with. You want to be fair in your evaluation and not have too many personal issues seep into the evaluation. Ask your fellow lawyers how they evaluated their paralegals; there may be a form your firm wants you to use. Some factors that most companies evaluate paralegal on are: Did the paralegal work as a team player? Did they gather the necessary information? Are they familiar with the specific assignments and can they perform within the specialty? Did they solve problems practically? Were they on time with due dates? Did they handle clients properly? Are their writing assignments clear, concise and accurate? and Does the paralegal meet or exceed the minimum billable hours?

The most important factor is if the paralegal's work is compatible to the work you expect and do. Did he/she become your right hand man and a friend to the clients? Did the paralegal's work closely match yours and can you combine the two. It's fine to show how the assignment should be completed, but did you have to review the basics issues of their work. This may have been too much work for you and was unnecessary if the paralegal is the right one. Paralegals are there to get things done, and to solve issues. They should not create problems or give you more work.

Work with the Paralegal

Paralegals can save you and the firm a lot of time and money while maintaining good client relations. The major advantage that paralegals can bring to your practice makes it very advisable to learn to work with them. You and your fellow associates may feel you are utilizing paralegals to the best of their ability, but the paralegals may have a different opinion. You may be unaware of you firm's unwitting participation to hamper paralegal growth. Try to foster the best possible relationship with your paralegals. This will only help your firm since utilizing paralegals often means more cost-efficient bills and happier clients. And when clients are happy, success for the firm follows.

You are somewhat accountable for the success or failure of paralegals' performance. This might be hard to comprehend but it is true. It is your overall responsibility to give your client the best possible service. In order to do this you must make all parts of your team work to full potential. Communication is the key. You must be able to communicate what you want in an open, friendly manner. Paralegals must be given clear ideas as to what is expected of them.

Plan time to thoroughly explain each new assignment, they may not know the difference between wanting to learn and what and how to learn. Bear in mind generation differences. Ask paralegals about their other skills, listen to what they tell you and intertwine these areas with your practice. Find out where they need training. If you become a counsel, offer training and provide necessary support to achieve success.

Legal Secretaries

The profession of legal secretary has been around almost as long as lawyers. There were legal secretaries in England three and four hundred years ago, known as clerks. They copied the results of lawsuits and other legal matters while their bosses, the barristers and lawyers, went about their legal business. In essence, these clerks were lawyers in training or apprentice lawyers.

The specific duties of a legal secretary will generally include correspondence, pleadings at the direction of the legal assistant/paralegal or attorney. They also see that court documents are filed properly, on time, and in the correct court. They keep the legal calendar for the attorney, proofread documents for factual, grammatical and typographical errors and make corrections, maintain files, and handle phone calls.

If you are a tax attorney, your legal secretary can prepare tax returns for your clients, keep up with tax law, and contact clients under your supervision. In estate and trusts law they can help you prepare wills, prepare final tax returns for the estate of a deceased, contact those named in the will and help with other tasks. In real estate law your legal secretary can ensure that the title search, appraisal, and deed are accurate, copy file documents, and perhaps participate in the actual closing. In corporate law they can help you draft contracts and other corporate documents. In criminal law they can help you field the calls of people who have just been arrested and assist you in preparing the necessary paperwork for release.

In a solo law firm a legal secretary may have the responsibility for all the administrative tasks, which almost certainly includes some accounting functions. You may start to place a great deal of trust in your legal secretary's ability to perform daily business if you are a solo lawyer. If you work in a large law firm you may have a legal secretary who performs and coordinates law office activities and makes sure that information is sent in a timely fashion to staff and clients.

In a solo law firm a legal secretary may have the responsibility for all the administrative tasks, which almost certainly includes some accounting functions. You may start to place a great deal of trust in your legal secretary's ability to perform daily business if you are a solo lawyer. If you work in a large law firm you may have a legal secretary who performs and coordinates law office activities and makes sure that information is sent in a timely fashion to staff and clients.

Know the Power of the Paralegal or Secretary

When working with secretaries and paralegals, it is always important to know who has influence over important partners. Often legal secretaries have great working relationships with the partners they assist and can be a valuable ally. Other times an attorney's secretary can be difficult to work with and can damage your relationship with colleagues. This is especially true at smaller firms where secretaries and paralegals have more responsibility and there is a closer working relationship between all the members of the firm.

For example, at one small firm, there was only one legal secretary. She managed the office and had a lot of power over the day-to-day business of the firm. Because she was the only female in the firm, she established working relationships with only men. When a female junior associate came into the firm, they had a terrible time working together. The secretary would go into the entire associate's files and proofread her work. She would then correct the associate in front of the attorneys about the appropriate font styles to use and about any minor errors she could find.

The legal secretary did this under the guise of helping the associate become integrating into the firm, even though she had never checked over the work of anyone else. At first, the associate tried her hardest to win over the legal secretary, proofreading her work furiously. Unfortunately, the secretary found or made up all kinds of little errors in her work. Eventually, the associate began just ignoring the legal secretary, and not trying to spend any time near her. She began speaking with other attorneys directly when she could, and hid her electronic files from the legal secretary's view.

Eventually the associate realized that this legal secretary was out to discredit her. It was frustrating that she had to go to such lengths to please this secretary, while everyone else in the firm was treated well. The only way the associate was able to find harmony in her workplace was to not take the legal secretary's actions personally, and avoid her. After doing this, she was finally able to form successful relationships with the other attorneys in the office.

Conclusion

In this chapter you have learned how to deal with clients, colleagues and paralegals. Components for good client relations were discussed, such as technical and personal. You now have a better understanding of how to work with different types of clients.

Paralegals and legal secretaries can be a great asset to you. They can have different roles in different law firms. They can help you immensely if you work with them successfully. Accountability for paralegal performance lies with you. It is your responsibility to see that your client receives the highest quality service possible. To make that happen it is necessary to see that all parts of the delivery system are in top shape and working order.

Paralegals need skill training and you need to know how to train and delegate the work. Be aware of the wide range of expertise paralegals bring to the workplace. Just because they may have only a few years of legal experience does not dismiss the value they bring.

This chapter also gave you helpful questions to ask yourself before leaving a position like: "Can I get to where I want to be from this position?" It enables you to know when and why you should leave a position and how to ensure a successful transition

As a new lawyer you now know more about the politics of a law firm and how you have to behave to succeed in it. This chapter discussed different ways that you can handle difficult colleagues, especially partners. You now know the best ways to handle these situations and why. You were given steps on how to interact successfully with client and colleagues such as talking to a colleague privately about a problem, and you now know how to portray yourself for overall success.

Chapter Nine

Make the Law Firm Work For You

As a new associate you are going to have to make the firm work for you. In order to do the best you must conform to the firm's procedures. You are the new person and your first priority should be to fit into the firm in order to get the experience you want. By not abiding by firm policy you make yourself appear as an outsider, who doesn't quite fit in or thinks they are above the rules. Remember you must strive to achieve a healthy working relationship within the framework of the firm and be thought of as a "team player."

Within any law firm there are norms, procedures and groups. It is helpful to understand this informal staff organization when trying to understand the relationships within the law firm. There are a number of bases for staff grouping, including status in the company, sex, attitudes, seniority, and common interests and activities. Most lawyers belong to several overlapping groups. Different groups have different degrees of prestige and authority within the firm. Entrance into the top group in a law firm may take years, if ever accomplished and it is usually gained when you become a senior partner yourself. How much money and clients you bring into the firm will also help you break into the top group.

To become a member of a group involves identifying group expectations and then trying to meet them. A group of new associates all have similar expectations so you probably will find acceptance into a group of your peers most easily. However you should always try to break into the more senior groups where you will meet and connect with the people who can help you obtain your goals.   Being involved in a group can help you handle many issues, but be careful, if proper interaction is not done it can cause you problems.

Below are some self-evaluating questions that will help you better understand the more common practices that occur in your relationships with colleagues. As you answer, think about whether each statement reflects an expectation you hold for your colleagues. After you finish, evaluate your answers. Note where you may need to work on your relationships. Try to put yourself on the receiving side of these statements. Would you like these things done to you? What would you do it they were done to you? How would they affect your relationships?

1. Am I considerate of my fellow colleagues?
2. Do I gossip about my colleagues and clients?
3. Do I interfere in other's work?
4. Do I complain about my duties?
5. Do I criticize any previous lawyer's achievement?
6. Am I sympathetic to others?
7. Do I expect things done my way?
8. Am I constantly talking about how things should be done?
9. Do I belittle my co-workers?
10. Do I compete ethically?

Yes, realistically as an associate you will want to become a partner. But you will have to prove you are worthy of this position in a professional as well as social way. Make a good analysis of the law firm you are in. Learn how the partners got there and ask yourself if that is the way you want to make partnership. Most of the time, good ethics and just plain good relationship practices get you what you want. You are going to have to live with yourself even after you make partnership. So analyze how and what you will have to do to become a partner.

Optimism

Be optimistic! How successful you become could depend in part on your general outlook on life. Those who generally expect good things to happen are more likely than negative people to achieve their goals. An optimist will try to overcome obstacles when confronted with impediments, whereas pessimists are more likely to cease striving because pessimist have less favorable views about how things will turn out.

Consider your own general outlook. Do you believe that most situations will turn out in your favor? Do you strive to produce desired results before circumstances get out of hand? If you cannot answer these questions in a positive manner you might try substituting positive forecasts for those situations in which you predict bad outcomes. Making sure to plan ahead and, keeping a list of all the good things that happen are useful tactics to gaining greater optimism.

An optimist appears to be self-confident, positive and in a good mood. We tend to believe what people tell us about themselves with their body language and self-confidence is a powerful social signal. Unless we have a specific reason to suspect otherwise, we assume the optimist's self-confidence is a product of competence. So not only do we like optimists, they can sometime appear more competent. Clients do not understand the law and that is why they hired you. Appearance, attitude and how you carry yourself are the most crucial factors in determining how they evaluate you.

Perfect this positive personality technique. It will combat and heal the any complaining traits you may have developed. Complaining is a form of pessimistic behavior. Try to solve your complaining problem with a positive act. For example, instead of complaining about the way that things are done, make the procedure work for you. Instead of complaining about the secretary, sit down and explain what you want done in a way to make sure he or she can do it. Be positive and use the procedures of the firm to your best advantage, don't try to change them or complain about them.

Remember that people are comfortable with what they know. They will feel uncomfortable with you if you try to change their long-standing procedures or change their familiar ways. People tend to get into a certain accepted routine. They have learned not to question and may not even notice things that will be blatantly obvious to you as a newcomer. You will wonder why these obvious things are not complained about by the people that have been there for a while. You will soon find out that there is a good reason why no one seems to notice them. The reason is, if you notice and complain you will get into more trouble than it is worth. Some things in a law firm are not debatable, so no one mentions them.

Never complaining negatively, however, is different than taking initiative with a case and showing off your brilliant legal ideas or solutions. If you have a great idea on how to address a legal issue, or a better way to meet a client's needs, definitely talk to a senior attorney about it- that is what sets you apart from the rest. Just remember to always be solution focused. Go into a senior attorney's office with a way to make something better. Never go in with a problem you don't already have a solution for. Senior attorneys have their own work and are very busy. No one appreciates complaints that will only give them more work, such as how the filing system is terrible or how the cases are assigned unfairly. Anything that you can easily work around without negatively affecting your work for the client, do so. No one will tell you this, you would have to find it out the hard way.

People don't like to hear the negative comments especially about their work. Some coworkers may make your negative comment seem like evidence of you're neurotic or worrier type personality. That makes them feel and look better, while you look bad. If you voice the negative you may not seem like a team player because bringing up negative possibilities can deflate the enthusiasm of the group that is supposed to be excited about whatever project they are working on. People tend to see anxiety and even a tendency to question as a sign of weakness and indecision. People want leaders who are confident, optimistic and bold. They also want messages that are simple and direct.

Just as a positive mood in other people can elicit a positive mood in us, a pessimist's anxiety and negativity may taint our interactions with others. Seeing someone in a pessimistic and negative mood may only make others feel the same way. You don't want to be associated with negative feelings.

Positive Attitude and Complaining

Complaining in a law firm is quite troublesome and is to be avoided. If you absolutely need someone to talk to, save it for your friends and family There is really no room for complaining by a new associate in a law firm. For the most part complaining will only hurt you mentally, physically, socially and financially. It will most likely not get you what you want from the law firm. You must use a different method if want to achieve your goal.

If the issue is not something that can be resolved on its own, think carefully about whether or not it is worth complaining to others about. If the issue is in reference to a particular case, first, try to go to the person who is causing the problem. If you delineate the issue in a professional manner, it appears that you are just being conscientious and not truly complaining.

If the issue involves personal matters, it becomes more difficult. First try to handle it yourself between you and the other person. If this doesn't work, you can't ignore it and you really need to get it resolved, then you might want to approach an office manager or administrator. They are sometimes very helpful, and may be able to work out some arrangement with you that avoids the reputation of being a complainer. If this does not work, then you might be forced to speak to a senior associate, and then possibly a partner, if the problem persists. This method is reserved for major issues that cannot be resolved by anyone else. Try not to go this far, as these means are to be used only in extreme cases. The best solution is to handle it yourself.

It is important to remember that no one likes a complainer, no one wants to work with a complainer, and it could seriously hurt your career to be considered someone that people cannot rely on to do a job effectively without issue. In the legal profession especially, you need to appear to be self-sufficient and competent to handle the problems that occur. If you complain to someone that is more senior than you, it almost always appears that you cannot handle the job yourself and that person will be less-inclined to pass along future case work to you. This is especially true with older partners. The key to effective, positive complaining is being solution focused. Never address a problem without already coming up with a possible solution and a way to implement it.

Please remember that every job has ordinary annoyances that come with working with a group of diverse people. It is important for you to have a support network at your firm in order to deal with every day office problems. Often a good working relationship with fellow associates or paralegals is very important. Have an ally in as many people in the firm as you can. It is basic human nature that people will be more willing to help someone that has acted as a friend. Likewise, if you have the opportunity to do a favor for someone else, you should always do it. You never know when that person may be able to help you with an issue that you have.

There is also the risk of a person being too optimistic. Some optimists may mildly distort reality. These people may believe that even though there was an eight person team working on a case it was primarily their input and efforts that pulled in the positive results. Or maybe their self worth issues interfere with relationships with their clients. For example; one attorney assumed his client rejected his law proposal because the client had bad decision making techniques. Instead, he should have realized that it was his failure to explain and design a proposal that reflected what the client wanted that caused the rejection. He did not work effectively with the client and he reached an inappropriate conclusion. The client's evaluation of his work didn't lower his self-evaluation, just his opinion of the client. Optimism is a good quality to have but don't let it interfere with your ability to know when you need improvement.

Also, continually pointing out your accomplishment, bragging or trying to convince others of your worth dilutes the positive feeling you receive from an accomplishment.   The more you brag about how good you are the more others will start to avoid you, talk behind your back about your insecure need to brag, and perhaps even resent you. Don't confuse self-confidence and an optimistic outlook with bragging.

There can be some pitfalls to being an optimist. Key into your personality to find if you are unrealistically optimistic. Do you over emphasize the importance of your contributions, ignoring or discounting criticism? Do not become overly positive with your self worth. If you rely to heavily on self-enhancement and self-protection techniques you run the risk of becoming unaware of true feedback that you can learn from.

How Pessimism Can Work For You

Strategies need to fit the person. There may be some genetic influence on your disposition, There is evidence that suggests that genes play a role in the development of optimism and pessimism. You may be a pessimist at heart and optimism may not work for you all the time. You may be able to change to an optimistic attitude only up to a certain point and then your pessimistic nature kicks in. If you try to deny your pessimistic nature, it may cause you more anxiety and have a detrimental effect on your career. Pessimism can be a good thing if you handle it right. You can use your pessimistic thinking and transform anxiety into action.

Pessimists tend to dwell on all that can go wrong and have a low prediction of the outcome. In order to make pessimism work for you, review all the outcomes for the upcoming situation. Spend a lot of time mentally going through the possibilities until you have a clear idea of everything that you need to do in order to have the best shot at success. Take control of both your anxiety and the situation by focusing on the potential downside and prepare for anything that you feel may hinder the success of the event. Learn to manage your pessimistic anxiety so that it doesn't keep you from doing what you need to do. Do your best to anticipate pitfalls and then fend off any disasters that you could foresee. Take control of the pessimistic thoughts and turn them around before they become a reality.

You might be anxious about a brief you have prepared and have a low expectation about the outcome. If you make your pessimistic thoughts work for you by thinking about everything that could be wrong with it and fixing them, then you have made your negative thoughts produce positive results. Your brief should now be as perfect as you can make it.

Some pessimists fall into the trap of blaming others for things that don't go well. Surely there are times when other people and or circumstances contribute to your problems, but it is you who must rise to the occasion and take responsibility for your own failures. Circumstances don't make a person. This doesn't mean that you shouldn't hold people accountable for their actions, but make sure that you hold yourself accountable for your own reactions to other people and circumstances around you.

Jim is a typical associate that fell into this trap. Jim works in a large law firm. He worked with a team on an important case. He did his part in collecting the information and providing his best techniques in handling the case. After all the information was gathered and the best techniques decided on there was new information found that brought a new light on how the case should be handled. Jim was very upset that all his work was in vain and started to blame his fellow colleagues for their inadequacies in not finding this information sooner. He felt powerless over handling the case and frustrated with his team. The other members felt he was not a team player and did not want to work with him.

If Jim hadn't blamed others and took control over the situation and just change the techniques instead of complaining and blaming his fellow colleagues, he would have regained his control. He would have played a key role in creating his own success. He could have shown the others that he could bounce back, even under adversity. Blaming others takes an enormous amount of mental energy. It's a "drag me down" mind set that creates stress. Blaming makes you feel powerless over your own success because it is contingent on the actions and behavior of others, which you can't control. Make sure you avoid the same mistakes in your own career.

Pessimism or Optimism

Most of us are a combination of pessimist and optimist, but we tend to lean toward one or the other. If you are not sure if you typically use pessimistic or optimistic strategies, here is a little questionnaire that will help you determine what you most likely are. Choose the response that most fits what you would do.

Optimism/ Pessimism Quiz

1 The case you are in charge of is a great success.
   a. Everyone worked hard on the case
   b. Because I scrutinized everyone's work

2. You and your coworker make up after a fight.
   a. I forgave him/her
   b. I had to be forgiven

3. You get lost driving to a client's house.
   a. My client gave me the wrong directions
   b. I misunderstood the directions

4. Your spouse gives you a gift for no occasion.
   a. He /she just got a new job
   b. I bought him/her something last week

5. You forgot your best friend's birthday.
   a. I know my friend doesn't mind

b. I'm not good at remembering birthdays

6. You get a compliment from a coworker who admires you.
   a. I am a well-liked person
   b. I am appealing to her/ him

7. You run for president of an important club and you win.
   a. I work very hard at everything I do
   b. I have a lot of experience and worked very hard in the club

8. You miss an important appointment.
   a. I sometimes forget things
   b. I should have checked my appointment book

9. You run for president of an important club and you lost.
   a. I didn't campaign enough
   b. The person who won knew more people

10. You gave a great party at your home for all the firm's staff.
    a. I am a good host
    b. I was in an extraverted mood that night

11. You stop a car from being stolen by calling the police.
    a. An unusual group of people around the car caught my eye
    b. I was alert that day

12. You buy your spouse a gift and he/she doesn't like it.
    a. He/she is hard to buy for
    b. I didn't think long enough about what they wanted

13. You gain weight after a cruise and can't lose it.
    a. The diet I tried didn't work
    b. Most diets don't work

14. Your real-estate broker makes you a lot of money.
    a. My real-estate broker is a top-notch investor

b. My real-estate broker decided to do something new

15. You win a tennis match.
   a. I trained very hard
   b. I was feeling like a winner

16. You lose an important case.
   a. I didn't prepare well
   b. I wasn't as smart as the other lawyers

17. You don't get enough notice to finish doing the research for a case, you somehow get it done.
   a. I am an efficient person
   b. I am a good lawyer

18. You lose a tennis match, for which you have been training a long time.
   a. I'm not good at that sport
   b. I'm not very athletic

19. Your cell phone battery goes dead just when you need to use it.
   a. The phone never worked well
   b. I didn't check the battery

20. You lose you temper with a client.
   a. He/she was in a bad mood
   b. He/she was constantly calling me for the same information

21. You pay a late fee for not paying your credit card on time.
   a. I was lazy about paying my bill this month
   b. I always put off paying my credit cards

22. You ask your attractive neighbor out to dinner and he/ she says no.
   a. I didn't ask him/her the right way
   b. I wasn't myself that day

23. You are picked from a crowd of people to answer a question and be on a TV show.
    a. I looked the most attentive
    b. I was in the right place at the right time

24. You save a child from drowning
    a. I know what to do in a crisis
    b. I know CPR

Count how many "a" answers you have. The answer "a" tends to be optimistic answers and the answer "b" tends to be pessimistic answers. If you answered "a" in 18 to 24 questions, you are very optimistic. If you answered "a" in 12 to 18, you are moderately optimistic. If you answered "a" in 6 to 12 you are moderately pessimistic and if you answered "a" in less then 6 you are very pessimistic.

We have to learn to trust our innate personality as to whether optimism or pessimism works for us in the work place. As a new lawyer you have to learn to recognize these characteristics in others and learn to work with them.

Negotiations Between Optimists and Pessimists

You have to find ways to negotiate different solutions to potential clashes between your own preferred strategy and the strategy of co-workers or clients. Especially when one person has authority over you, the distinction between what you do privately in your head and what you express aloud can have dramatic effects.

A simple solution is to have an optimistic person do more of the staff management and client socializing. This makes use of the optimist's positive and uplifting personality. If you are an optimist personality, capitalize on it and use it to help you get ahead in the firm.

If you tend to be more of a pessimist, learn not to flood your team with negative scenarios. Instead work through your conflicts by yourself first, and only then gently bring up the negative possibilities if you perceive them as likely to be of real concern. Learn to pass on the benefits of your negative thinking without infecting others with anxiety. If you are not sensitive to the effects of negativity on other people, you may end up with coworkers not appreciating your strengths because your negativity overwhelms everything else.

Look Within Yourself

Everyone has some traits in their personality that may hinder their ability to have the firm work for them. You may have subconscious attitudes that may hinder you from using the law firm to its best advantage. It is useful to look within your own personality to find out what coping mechanism you use and if it is working. Most of us get into bad habits when we deal with stressful situation. We may overreact, blow things out of proportion, or focus on the negative. When you are irritated, annoyed, and bothered, you may act in a way that might actually stop you from getting the result you want. You can't think clearly under those conditions.

When you are in an anxious situation at work, what do you do? Do you tend to want to avoid it, lower your expectations, procrastinate, or do you justify your performance in a way that will make it less incriminating if the performance does not go well. Are you a perfectionist who has to have things done a certain way, better then it already is being done? Do you use strategies like compassion to understand the situation? Do you carefully choose your battles? Do you please the important partners in the firm?

If you attempt to manage your anxiety by avoiding the things that make you anxious, it may be effective for a time, but ultimately you will be disappointed. If you are cautious, you will have fewer episodes of anxiety that precede a particular event. Overall unfortunately, you will probably still be anxious because you may find yourself being constantly alert to a potential situation that will cause you risk. You may want to leave a law firm because you can't avoid the anxious situations any longer. Facing the anxious causing situation and finding a way to deal with the stress might be the better choice.

Do you lower your expectations by telling yourself ninety percent of the lawyers in this firm don't make partners so I probably won't? By lowering your expectation you have taken some of the pressure off but did you really help yourself make the firm work for you? Instead look around and find out what that ten percent had that got them their partnership.

Are you using procrastination as an excuse? Are you always stressed and behind schedule. As deadlines approach, do you stay up all night frantically trying to get everything done. Are you least likely to be working on the project that is closest to being due? Do you feel you have too much work? Typically do you hand in something at the last minute that you put together quickly because you didn't have enough time to do your best work. If so, you may have doubts as to whether you are intelligent, creative, and capable enough to do consistently good work. Are you just trying to provide yourself with an out? If your proposal does not pass muster at work, it is not because you lack creativity or ability, you can say it is just because you threw it together at the last minute. But aren't you denying yourself the right to know how good you really are?

If you are a perfectionist you are engaged in a losing battle. If you focus on what's wrong with the way the firm does things and you need to fix it, this implies that you are dissatisfied and discontent. If things should be done the perfect way or more specifically your way then you are in for a problem. Try to realize that while there's always a better way of doing something, this doesn't mean that you can't accept and appreciate good in the way things already are being done.

Using these and other avoidance techniques hinder you from taking advantage of opportunities or creating prospects in the law firm. You will not utilize clear feedback about your work so that you can grow and learn. You will be unlikely to develop the confidence that comes from knowing precisely how to bring about a successful outcome. Those who are most knowledgeable and skilled are aware of their weaknesses, and that awareness makes authentic confidence.

Certain strategies such as compassion can help you alleviate the stressful situations and get you the result you desire. The old adage is especially true in a law firm: if you put yourself in the other person's shoes than you can understand why they are acting the way they are. When you understand them, you are more likely to handle them in the most successful way. You must recognize that other people's problems, their pain and frustration, are just as important as yours. When you understand where people are coming from, what they are trying to say, and what's important to them, than you will be able to successfully handle a client as well as your co-workers.

Do you choose your battles wisely in the firm? Working in a firm is filled with choices between making a big deal out of something or simply letting it go. There will be times when you will want or need to argue, confront, or even fight for something you believe in. However don't ague, confront or fight over just anything- do so only for the most crucial issues. There will always be people who disagree with you, people who do things differently, and cases that don't work out. If you always fight against them you are not going to be happy in the firm and the firm is not going to be happy with you. If you choose your battles wisely you'll be far more effective in winning those that are truly important.

Who Do You Please

You can't please all of the people all of the time so just please the important people in the firm. One of the first things you should do when you get a position in a firm is to find out who the senior partners are and how you can please them. Ascertain their beliefs, attitudes, and quirks and abide by them. The sooner you accept the fact that you are not going to be able to please everyone in the firm, the sooner you will be able to key in on the important people that you need to please.

When good events happen in the firm use optimistic techniques to describe them in a positive way. If you believe that good events in the firm have controlled causes then you will be able to see your success in the firm as within your grasp. Here are some situations where you should use optimistic techniques to achieve success. If you are up for a promotion, writing a difficult report, leader of a team etc. you have control over presenting them in an optimistic way for success.

Use the principals that will get you the best results. Whatever strategy you use will get you the result that it represents. If you are in the habit of being uptight whenever work isn't quite right, repeatedly react to criticism by defending yourself, insisting on being right, allowing your thinking to snowball in response to adversity, your work in the firm will reflect that. However if you choose to use compassion, choose your battles wisely, please the most important people in the firm and use other like strategies then your position in the firm will work for you.

Opportunities

Recognizing opportunities also plays a major role in success. Sometimes you will find yourself in the right place at the right time and knowing and using that opportunity successfully will improve your chances of success within the firm. It's not a matter of getting more or better opportunities than others, it's simply recognizing and exploiting the opportunities that you do get. You should key in to self-awareness, networking, and positioning.

The best way to find opportunities is to make them yourself. The surest way to find opportunities is to work in a firm where you already know people, preferably partners. Of course there is always the element of luck. Some people will just be in the right place at the right time in the right firm. But one has to be aware and alert to these opportunities.

Achieving your Plans and Goals

A law firm can't read your mind, supervisors are not aware of your inner most desires and motivation unless you make it known what you want. Alerting the firm to your goals involves finesse, awareness of office politics and motivation. But first determine what you want. You may want to advance on a vertical climb or you may not wish to move up the ladder at all rather expanding horizontally. Sometimes all it takes is alerting a partner in the correct manner, and you can find yourself with all the types of cases you want, working with the people you want.

When you are ready you may have to ask for advancement in a manner that is appealing to the firm and non-threatening. Try to find out the best policy that works in the firm and to whom to go to. Here are a few general techniques that you can used:

1. Get sociable with the key people
2. Make your goals know even if you have to write a proposal
3. Get some kind of recognition to make the firm proud of you
4. Learn from your colleagues the best way to work with difficult partners
5. Make sure you complete and satisfy equitable partners' requests.

Balance

Many lawyers find that having interests outside their work develops and maintains total well being. Balance in work, social and leisure activities is essential to personal and professional growth. The impact of too much or too little attention to any area can spill over and produce negative consequences in the other areas. The lawyer who works day and night can destroy family life and important relationships. The lawyer who relies solely on work for a sense of personal worth may act resentfully toward colleagues and clients who fail to meet his expectations. In fact, any negative experience on the job could have far-reaching impact if the job is that lawyer's whole life.

No formula is available regarding the amount of time you should devote to work versus your social life. What is required for a healthy balance will vary from person to person. You must find your happy balance by trial and error. If you find that work related activities are interfering with your family life to a stressful point, then you are devoting too much energy to work related activities and you should change your habits.

While working on a case you will find at different times you can devote more time to social activities, but at others times you must devote time to the case. This is one of the advantages of the legal profession. Make the most of the time you have to spend on your social life when you can. Try to anticipate when you will have free time and plan to have it work for you, in order to refresh and revitalize.

How To Achieve Career Satisfaction As a Lawyer

Express your own values and notions of right and wrong. You should be conscious of the way your legal training can negatively impact your personal life, and make sure to preserve time for yourself, your family, your hobbies and for contribution to your community. If your current position does not fit your personality, your skills or your interests find one that does. Look at these career developments as a process.

Resist pressure to conform to a style of lawyering unsuitable to you, or that violates your senses of fair play and diplomacy. Be conscious of the way your legal training can negatively impact your personal life. Lawyers are trained to separate their feelings from the position the clients want them to take. This is a good strategy for your professional life, but it might negatively impact you emotionally. Recognize that your ultimate goal in life is to enjoy the process by placing as much emphasis on qualities of affection and well being as on influence, skill, responsibility and wealth. You will likely have to sacrifice some money in order to do this but the inner satisfaction you receive in the long run will pay off.

If your current position doesn't fit your personality, your skills or your interests, find another one. What good is money if you are miserable throughout the day? Career development is a process and each position is a stepping stone toward the right job for you. Don't expect your first job out of law school to represent the ideal job. Approach your early years in the legal profession with patience, it will take two or three years at least before your find your right niche, but the search is worth it.

Conclusion

You are going to have to make the law firm work for you. This chapter has explained many aspects that will enable you to succeed in doing this. Some ways mentioned were by conforming to the firm's policies, successfully interacting with coworkers and clients, pleasing the important partners, and analyzing your own defense mechanisms.

In any law firm there are norms, procedures and groupings. By identifying and then meeting group expectations you now know the basics of staff groupings and how to achieve successful entrance into the best group for you and why this is important. You were given some self-evaluating questions to enlighten you on some of the successful interaction with colleagues and clients. Also you were able to find out whether you were prone toward optimism or pessimism and how to make each personality trait work for you within the firm.

How successful you become could depend in part on your general outlook on life. If you expect good things to happen it is more likely that they will. You analyzed your own general outlook and you were given ideas on how to make it work best for you within the firm. If you were mostly pessimistic you were given strategies such as reviewing all the possible outcomes until you have a clear idea of everything that you need to do in order to have the best shot at success. Prepare for anything that you feel may hinder your success. These types of strategies were given in order to help you turn your pessimism into positive reactions. You were also given techniques in reacting to co-workers and clients who may clash with your type of personality. Simple solutions such as having the optimist handle the socializing were given.

You were also given insights into how you handle stressful situations and how these affects the firm's working for you. Coping mechanism such as avoidance, procrastination, disorganization and others were disclosed and successful solutions were given. Compassion, choosing your battles wisely, pleasing the most important people in the firm and using other like strategies were discussed.

How to recognize, develop and make opportunities in a law firm was given. Self-awareness, networking and positioning were reviewed in the opportunity process. Of course the end result of the information in this chapter is to create a balanced life that you have made through working in a law firm that you enabled to work for you.

"For anyone contemplating becoming a Lawyer..."

So You Want To Be A
Lawyer?

Official
Know-It-All
Guide

Marianne Pilgrim Calabrese
Susanne Mary Calabrese

Chapter Ten

The Ten Commandments of a Lawyer

The Ten Commandments of a Lawyer

1. Work under partners who like you.
2. Balance your personal and professional life.
3. Don't alienate any clients.
4. Work for the right size and type firm to achieve your goals.
5. Work In the area of law you find interesting.
6. Use legal secretaries and paralegal effectively.
7. Follow established polices and procedures of the firm.
8. Always have a professional attitude.
9. Bill hours to clients effectively.
10. Don't alienate any colleagues

1. Work under partners who like you.

Remember that partners, especially senior partners are the most important people in the firm. Not only do they set the tone of the firm, but also they have the power to hire and fire. Partners can easily make your life wonderful or miserable. Your first commandment is to work under a partner who likes you. This is the number one thing you need in order to succeed in a law firm. In fact, it is probably the only thing you need. You can have everything else but if you don't have the partners' favor then unfortunately you have nothing.

The easiest way to become a favorite is to know someone, preferably an equity partner in the firm. You should try all your connections when looking for a position and if you land a position where you know people, you are ahead of the game. If, however, you find yourself in a firm where you do not know anyone, you will have to do a little work socializing in order to gain a popular spot.

If you are not working under a partner that you know or in a law firm where you have connections, it can sometimes be hard to get to the partners and form a bond. First if you do a good job, bring in money and clients, you will quickly gain popularity. If you find yourself working for a difficult or distant partner, working directly with their secretary or paralegal is usually the easiest and most efficient way of connecting.

Social acceptance is something needed to work in any firm. You must strive to be socially accepted, especially by the partners. You may be great at your job but you need to be accepted by the partners; they have to feel they can work with you. In order to be accepted you must follow certain rules to survive in the system. Always agree with the partners, especially with the equity partners. Choose your clique of associates or partners and socialize with them. Don't do another associate's job unless the partner in charge asks you to and don't complain to a partner about another associate. Learn the best way to communicate with the equity partners. These are the things no one wants to tell you, but they do go on in a law firm and you will have to learn to deal with them to survive. (Refer to Chapter 7 and 8.)

2. Balance your personal and professional life.

Many lawyers find that having interests outside their work develops and maintains total well being. Balance in work, health, social and leisure activities is essential to personal and professional growth. The impact of too much or too little attention to any area can spill over and produce negative consequences in the other areas. The lawyer who works day and night can destroy family life or important relationships. The lawyer who relies solely on work for a sense of personal worth may act resentfully toward colleagues and clients who fail to meet his expectations. In fact, any negative experience on the job could have a far-reaching impact if the job is that lawyer's whole life.

No formula is available regarding the amount of time you should devote to work versus social activities. What is required for a healthy balance will vary from person to person. You must find your happy balance by trial and error. If you find that work related activities are interfering with your family life causing constant stress than you are devoting too much energy to work related activities and must make your life more balanced

While working in a firm, you will find that at certain times you can attend many social activities, while at others times you must devote yourself entirely-to a case. This is one of the advantages of the legal profession if you can recognize it. Make the most of the time you have to spend on your social life when you can. Try to anticipate when you will have free time and plan to have it work for you, in order to refresh and revitalize.

Reserve time for yourself, your family, your hobbies and contribution to your community. You will likely have to sacrifice some money in order to do this but the inner satisfaction you receive in the long run will pay off. If your current position doesn't fit your personality, your skills or your interests, find another one. (Refer to Chapter 9)

Express your own values and notions of right and wrong. Resist pressure to conform to a style of lawyering unsuitable to you, or that violates your senses of fair play and diplomacy. Lawyers are trained to separate their feelings from the position the clients want them to take. This works well professionally but it may be bad for you emotionally. Look at the ultimate goal in life as enjoying the process. Place as much emphasis on affection and well -being as on influence, skill, responsibility and wealth. (Refer to Chapter 9)

3. Don't alienate any clients.

The ideal relationship with the client is to be his advocate and at the same time feel that justice is being served. Conflicts will arise in your career; on one side are your responsibilities to the clients and the legal system. On the other side are your own interests in remaining an upright person while earning a satisfactory living. The Rules of Professional Conduct prescribe terms for resolving some conflicts. All issues can be resolved through sensitive professional and moral judgment. There is no benefit to alienating a client, you must learn to deal with clients in a professional way.

There are basically two components to good client relations: technology and personality. The technical component consists of the procedures used to deliver the legal services in the case and the personal side is the verbal interaction between you and the client.

There are many ways to keep the technical side of your case running smoothly. Most importantly, keep your support team informed. Have backup support people and know how to get in touch with them at all times. Always know the status of the case and let your team know this information. Give clear assignments and deadlines. Also, make sure you communicate efficiently with your client. Know how much the case will cost and who and how to charge. Don't call meetings that will not result in a decision and keep deadline promises made to the client. Make sure the client's bill is prepared properly. It is sometimes a good idea to ask the client if you can meet them in their office so you can meet all the members of their team

The personal side of your career can also be enhanced with a few simple tips. Most importantly, only take a job or a case that you can do well in. If you make decisions about clients, during the initial interview decide if you can and want to handle a case. If you have agreed to accept representation, try to bond with the client. Treating the client with respect and keeping them happy is vital to your career. Explain fully your policy on fees. Always respond to telephone calls from the client, and always inform them of communications from your adversary. Every offer and counterproposal should be reviewed with the client. Never give the client the impression you are too preoccupied with other matters to devote whatever attention is necessary to his or her particular case. A large percentage of your success with a client has to do with the confidence and empathy you are able to instill.

Always do you homework before seeing a client; never give the impression that you have forgotten details previously furnished. Try to be compassionate, especially on cases that are emotional, for example divorce cases. Do not get involved with your clients that it will put you at risk of unquestionable actions. When the case is completed express you appreciation to the client.

Make sure you know whom your client is. When you work with in-house counsel, it is easy to mistake them for one of your team and to forget that, although they are working as attorneys for a company, they are also your clients. These attorneys pay the bill and are whom you are working for on a case.

If the client gets a little nasty, don't respond likewise back. Keep in mind this is an emotional experience for him. Don't over promise something you can't do or under deliver. Make clients feel important; the more important they feel the better they will feel about using you and referring you to their friends. (Refer to Chapter 8)

4. Work for the right size and type of firm to achieve your goals.

As a lawyer, you are likely to work in several different law firms over the course of your career. Even if you decide to stay in one firm, it is likely you will experience a series of changes within that firm. You can choose to work in a private practice, large, medium or small law firms, corporation, government, nonprofit, educational group, prepaid legal service or as an entrepreneur. You may find yourself in all of these types of settings during you career as a lawyer.

The right size and type of firm for your goals is determined by your outlook on environments such as working in a rural area, in suburban business districts, central business district, or only in certain cities. Do you want to be the owner, or mid level manager, supervised employee, part of a team, freelance? What compensation arrangements do you prefer- salaried, contingent, incentive bonus, share of profits, hourly, retainer, stock options, or commission? What size group is most comfortable to you- 5 to 15 people, 41 to 150 people or more then 150?

There are advantages and disadvantages of small firm in a small town vs. large firm in a large town. You also must consider the medium size firms in both large and small cities as a viable option that may incorporate some of the good and bad features of both large and small firms. The choice is not an easy one.

The type and size of the firm, the practice area, the geographic location and the attitudes of the lawyers at the firm will all have a large effect on your life, both at work and at home. Thus, it is important to find the right type and size law firm for you. You have to pick the environment that will work best for you. (Refer to Chapter 3.)

5. Work in the area of law you find interesting.

A law career is not a single skill career. It encompasses many different types of law with many roles performed within each. A lawyer may perform several different roles such as litigation, advocacy, negotiation and advising. Not only are there different roles in a particular law position but there are many different types of lawyers. Most lawyers specialize in some type of law, such as business, criminal, family, intellectual property, international, labor, property, public interest, taxation, tort, agriculture, aviation, sports election, maritime/admiralty, military and entertainment. You will have to make a decision about which type of law most interests you and what you are most skillful at.

Some roles you will be performing as a lawyer are advisor, mediator, evaluator, negotiator, advocate, agent, and fiduciary. Lawyer's can practice in transactional, representative, litigation, planning and preventive, education and adjudication roles. In the previous chapters, you have learned the different roles a lawyer plays and the different types of law you can practice in order to determine which suits you the best.

You will probably use all these roles to some extent in the legal profession. The kind of law you specialize in will determine which role you use the most. Decide which are your best skills and find out which type of law uses those skills the most. That will help you decide what kind of law you will want to specialize in. For example, if you love arguing a case and the drama of persuading people than a type of law that has a lot of trial work connected to it may suit you best.

As with all career paths, you should meet with a practicing attorney and talk about the aspects of any specialty you are considering. If possible, observe lawyers at work and ask yourself if the skills that they use are the skills that you have and enjoy working with. The type of law you practice will determine where the most openings are and how you should proceed in your job hunt. (Refer to Chapter 4)

6. Use legal secretaries and paralegals effectively.

As a lawyer, you will be doing a lot of work preparing for cases. Some of these tasks require your special knowledge of the law, while other aspects may be assigned to a paralegal or legal secretary. A paralegal can gather research information and sometimes pull all of the facts of the case together for you. Assembling and organizing background information and data that will support your case is their prime job. The paralegal has the primary responsibility of gathering any information relevant to the case.

Besides doing research and paperwork, a paralegal can interact with the client and other people involved in the case. You can also have a paralegal interview possible witnesses, write reports, draft documents, organize files, attend court proceedings, and assist you during a trial. When teamed with a lawyer, a paralegal can help with productivity by doing many hours of work at a reduced billing rate. Thus it is extremely cost effective to hire paralegal help.

The relationship between the client, paralegal, and you must be well defined. The client must be made aware that the paralegal is acting on your behalf and under your direction and that he/she is not a lawyer.

Paralegals can be given office duties too. They can organize employees, maintain the firm's financial files, and organize files on law guidelines and reference materials. Essentially they can be given non-clerical and non-secretarial legal work in assisting you. It is a good idea to set clear objectives for the paralegals but then allow them to complete the task on their own.

If you work with a somewhat inexperienced paralegal, who has been working only one or two years, you will have to determine which tasks they can perform the best. Most assignments you give should be research assignments. An experienced paralegal, one who has been working, five-years or more can be given more responsibility.

Paralegals can help you take on more cases. The specialized training paralegals receive, allows you to practice law and not get too bogged down in research and paper work. They will save you from having to do a huge amount of time-consuming groundwork.

Legal secretaries are also very helpful to a practicing attorney. The specific duties of a legal secretary will generally include correspondence, editing pleadings at the direction of the attorney and maintaining case files. They also see that court documents are filed properly, on time, and in the correct court. They keep the legal calendar for the attorney, proofread documents for factual, grammatical and typographical errors and make corrections, and handle phones.

There is no program that is right for all firms and legal departments. How the paralegals are used depend on the attitude of the firm. There are many issues that affect the attitude of the firm such as the ratio of paralegals to attorneys, which include practice specialties, level of assignments, number of years the firm has employed paralegals, acceptance of clients, billable rates, hiring criteria, job descriptions, turnover rate, profit margin, and incentives.

As a new associate, you will have to know how to utilize paralegals from the moment you enter the firm. You may have very different attitudes toward paralegals than the senior partners. Anyone who has worked in law for more than twenty years probably did not learn to utilize paralegals effectively. As a new associate you should expect paralegals to be part of the practice, the same as computers, secretaries and billable hours. Learn the procedures of the firm. Maybe the assigning of paralegals to attorneys is through a team or a pool. It really comes down to how your associate program is structured. You must conform to the program of your firm.

Although some firms may do it differently, it is generally more efficient to permanently assign paralegals to the same case or client matter throughout, rather than assign projects on a piecemeal basis. Otherwise, background information learned by paralegals and associates become fragmented and no one person knows enough details about the case. Too much time is wasted trying to bring new people up to date.

Paralegals can save you and the firm a lot of time and money while maintaining good client relations. The many advantages that paralegals can bring to your practice make it advisable to learn to work with them. Utilize paralegals to the best of their ability! (Refer to Chapter 8)

7.Follow established polices and procedures of the firm.

As a new associate you are going to have to make the firm work for you. In order to do that you have to conform to the firm's procedures. You are the new person and you are going to have to fit into the firm first in order to get the experience you need. Remember you must strive to achieve a healthy working relationship within the framework of the firm. You can't please all of the people all of the time, so just please the important people in the firm. One of the first things you should do when you get a position in a firm is to find out who the senior partners are and how you can please them. Ascertain their beliefs, attitudes, and quirks, then abide by them. The sooner you accept the fact becoming favored in the firm is essential, the sooner you will realize that you must be able to key in on the important people that you need to please.

ibilities can deflate the enthusiasm of the group that is supposed to
xcited about whatever project they are working on. People tend to
anxiety and even a tendency to question as a sign of weakness and
cision. People want leaders who are confident, optimistic and bold.
They also want messages that are simple, clear, and direct.
plaining in a law firm is quite difficult and is to be avoided. Save your
plaining for your friends and family if you absolutely need someone
lk to about it. There is really no room for complaining in a law firm
a new associate. For the most part, complaining will only hurt you
tally, physically, socially, and financially. It will not get you what
want from the law firm. Bringing a solution, and not a problem, to
eone in charge is often the best way to handle a problem.

Please remember that every job has ordinary annoyances that
e with working with a group of diverse people. It is important for
to have a support network at your firm in order to deal with every day
e problems. A good working relationships with fellow associates or
legals is very important. Have an ally in as many people in the firm as
can. It is basic human nature that people will be more willing to help
eone that has acted as a friend. Likewise, if you have the opportunity
a favor for someone else that is easily done, you should always do it.
never know when that person may be able to help you with an issue
you have.

Use the principals that compliment your personality best to attain
ofessional attitude. Different strategies work for each personality type.
ou are in the habit of being uptight whenever work isn't quite right,
repeatedly react to criticism by defending yourself, you insist on being
t, or you allow your thinking to snowball in response to adversity,
you must seriously try to recognize and combat these personality
s. Otherwise, your work in the firm will reflect your negative attitude.
ever if you choose to use compassion, choose your battles wisely,
se the most important people in the firm and use other like strategies,
your position in the firm will work for you. (Refer to Chapter9)

ll hours to clients' effectively.

Clients want to be treated fairly. Economics has forced clients to
me active, they want to do business with firms that not only produce

Being an associate is being smack in the middle of the soc
a firm . Within the attorneys employed you are on the bott
most dispensable member of the firm. As an associate, you
to demands from members above you, such as the senior a:
counsel, junior partners, partners and especially equity p;
quickest way to win favor is to make sure to bill enough hours
work look professional and try to bring in new clients.

In order to cope with the issues in the legal professi
have to learn the policies and procedures of the firm where y
an associate you will want to become a partner. You will h;
you are worthy of this position in a professional as well as
Make a good analysis of the law firm you are in. How did the
there and is that the way you want to make partnership? Mosl
good ethics and just plain good relationship qualities get yc
want. (Refer to Chapters 3, 6, 7, and 9.)

8. Always have a professional attitude.

Be optimistic! How successful you become could de
on your general outlook on life. Those who generally expect
to happen are more likely than less optimistic people to a
goals. An optimist will try to overcome obstacles when con
impediments, whereas pessimists are more likely to cease striv
they have less favorable views about how things will turn ou

An optimist appears to be self-confident, positive, ar
mood. We tend to believe what people tell us about themsel
confidence is a powerful social signal. Unless we have a speci
suspect otherwise, we assume the optimist's self-confidence is
competence. So not only do we like optimists, they can some
more competent. Clients do not understand the law and that
hired you. Appearance, attitude, and how you carry yourself
crucial factors in determining how they evaluate you.

People don't like to hear the negative comments, espe
their work. Some coworkers may interpret your negative
evidence of your neurotic or worrier personality. That mak¢
and look better, but makes you look bad. If you voice negativ
you may not seem like a team player because bringing

the best results but also have the lowest fees. Lawyers have learned to acknowledge this for survival.

When dealing with clients remember to be well aware of the billing practices employed by your firm. For example, there have been horror stories of law firm loosing big clients, not because clients were unsatisfied with an attorney's work, but because they were unwilling to pay for the services required. Your firm requires you to bill any time worked on a client's case and billing for this time is how your firm makes money. However, some clients will complain when they are billed for file organization, telephone conversations or other forms of advice. Make sure you know what the client will pay for and structure your billing of time accordingly. It will save you, and your client a lot of time, not to mention ill-will, if you do not have to fight over every minute the client will not pay for because you were not aware of the correct billing practices. (Refer to Chapters 6 and 8.)

10. Don't alienate any colleagues

Co- associates are important in meeting your social and office place needs, they are the primary source of advice and support. However, you are all in competition for partnerships and even though you are in the same boat, you must always act professionally. So keep this in mind and take this into consideration when working with them. You do not want to make enemies of your co-workers but you do not want them to take advantage of you either. You never know which ones may be your boss in the future.

There are certain steps you can take to ensure success when working with coworkers without alienating them. First, how you portray yourself has an overall effect on your success. Portray yourself as a positive, confident, and easygoing professional, even if you don't feel like it. If you appear nervous, angry, emotionally upset, hostile, or negative in any way, your chances of succeeding can decrease. The positive way you interact and respond to those in the firm will ensure your success. You have control over how you respond and react so you can control the situation.

There are some basic rules for interacting with your colleagues to ensure cohesive interaction, such as: Don't criticize or outwardly disagree with another associate in front of a client, talk to an associate privately about a problem. Choose your cliques of associates and socialize with them if possible. Don't do anyone else's job unless you are asked to by a partner. Reciprocate any favors that are given to you.

If you do have a confrontation with a co-worker, first try to listen to the facts without getting emotional. It is hard, but try to not take it personally. Skillful listening and feedback techniques will help you find the real problem. Your body posture, tone of voice and facial expression can all affect this. Look the person straight on, and at appropriate times stop talking and remain calm. Concentrate on what the person is trying to say. Add to the conversation things like: "If I understood you correctly you want..."

You have to acknowledge their emotions neutrally by letting them know you are trying to understand or that you do understand. Apologize if you think it is warranted or if not, try to compromise by using neutral statements such as: "I'm sorry this happened or I'm sorry you are upset with my assignment results. I understand how you have reached that conclusion. However, let me present a different interpretation of the data." If you want to reach an agreement, try statements like: "What is the next step? What do you think is a fair way to settle this? Let's try this to get it settled." "Let me give you a different perspective on that." Ultimatums are not a good idea. They usually are not effective and usually cause more harm than good.

Some good advice when dealing with other attorneys is that you can never judge the intelligence or importance of a lawyer on first glance. When working with them, or against them, never underestimate their legal cunning or importance in the firm. As a junior associate, beware of those associates that are only a year or two more senior than you. The profession of law attracts many people who like to be in charge and enjoy delegating responsibility to others. Never forget that some of these associates may be partners in the near future.

As a new attorney you will have to learn to work within the politics of the office. Most offices will be in the realm of normality and you will be able to ease into it. There will be, on rare occasion, where an experienced lawyer, maybe even a partner might be extra difficult to work with. This is not the occasional flare up or venting of emotions, it is the routine verbal battering by a firm member causing a chaotic environment and anxiety. The management usually tolerates their behavior because they hold an important position like equitable partner. Rarely is this behavior tolerated from someone who has no strong political or economic standing in the firm. The important lawyers who exhibit this behavior are usually excused or given slaps on the wrist or just labeled difficult to work with. You will have to learn how to handle them.

You will be able to recognize when a firm tolerates an extra difficult lawyer because instead of directly handling the person they will divert to other measures. They may move the lawyer to an office out of the mainstream, or they may tell you that it is just the way he is or he is just hard to work with. The difficult attorney may have constant turnovers of work mates such as secretaries. You may hear the management tell him he should not have yelled at an associate in the hallway, to do it in his office instead. Or you learn an administrator silently comforted an upset employee in hopes that the partners will talk to the offender. These are some signs to look for to identify a difficult lawyer. Learn from other employees' mistakes and follow your instincts when you see signs that this attorney is difficult to work with.

After you identify them then you know who to avoid working with if at all possible. If you can't avoid working with them and they are in a powerful position, try collaborating with their secretary of someone who knows how to handle them. (Refer to Chapters 7 and 8).

Conclusion

After reading this book you now are more aware of why you want to be a lawyer. You have considered the many issues of the legal profession before deciding. As a lawyer you will be guided by personal conscience as well as professional goals. Conflicts may arise between a lawyer's responsibilities to clients, to the legal system and to the lawyer's own interest in remaining an upright person while earning a satisfactory living. But all of these can be handled in a successful manner.

A legal career prepares you for an almost unlimited array of opportunities. Knowledge of the law is useful in most aspects of life and necessary in many. In a complex society contact with the law becomes increasingly more important. Your law degree uses are limited only by your own imagination and your awareness of the opportunities. You have chosen a career that will allow you to help the world while giving you a balanced happy life.

This book has shown you ways to know what you want from a law career and how to get it. Don't be afraid of change and believe in yourself. A career in law is a process and each position is a stepping stone toward the right job for you. Don't expect your first job out of law school to represent the ideal. Approach your early years in the legal profession with patience, it will take two or three years at least before your find your right niche, but the search is worth it!

Author's Biography

Marianne Pilgrim Calabrese earned her Masters Degree in Reading from Adelphi University. Her Bachelor degree from Queens College is in education and psychology. She is a published author and renowned artist. She has extensive classroom reading experience and has conducted workshops for the New York City Board of Education in Curriculum and testing. She is a former Director of the Nassau Reading Council, and has also received, "The Presidents' Club Award" from the International Reading association for her work.

To research her new book, Marianne spent many hours studying law-related books. She interviewed numerous lawyers and spent months researching different types of lawyers and firms. Marianne resides in Wellington, Fl.

Susanne Calabrese graduated with honors from the College of the Holy Cross with a B.A. in English and a focus on Pre-Law. She has worked for several years as a paralegal at a major law firm in Manhattan and San Diego, as well as at a small private practice on Long Island. She has experience in general litigation, securities litigation, real estate, medical malpractice, labor, employment, and immigration law. During her tenure as a paralegal, she has interviewed dozens of lawyers in all types of practice areas, researched the different employment opportunities and has seen first-hand what being a lawyer entails. Much of the research for this book comes from her personal career search. From her own recent experience taking the LSAT, researching law schools, preparing law school applications, applying for financial aid, investigating law curriculums, and then attending law school, she has accumulated a wealth of knowledge and helpful hints she shares with anyone considering this career path.

Bibliography

Arron, Deborah L, Running from the Law, Ten Speed Press, Berkeley, California , 1991

Carlson, Dr. Richard, Don't Sweat the Small Stuff and It's All Small Stuff, Hyperion, New York, 1997

Camenson, Blythe. Real People Working in Law, VGM Career Horizons, Lincolnwood, Illinois, 1997

Cefrey, Holly. Choosing a Career as a Paralegal , The Rosen Publishing Group, Inc., New York, 2001

Collins, Susan Ford, The Joy of Success, Harper Collins Publishers Inc. New York, NY, 2003

Edwards, Paul and Sarah, Changing Directions Without Losing Your Way, Putnam Inc. New York, 2001

Estrin B. Chere, Paralegal Career Guide, Wiley Law Publications, John Wiley & Sons, Inc. New York, 1996

Meyer, Jan, Career As A Lawyer, General Family Practice, Research No. 7..Careers Research Monographs, The Institute for Research, Chicago, 1998

Munneke, Gary, Careers in Law, VGM Career Horizons, Lincolnwood, Illinois, 1997

Munneke, Gary, Opportunities in Law Careers, VGM Career Horizons, Lincolnwood, Illinois, 1993

Bibliography

Norem, Julie K. Ph.D., The Power of Negative Thinking, Basic Books, 2001

A Career As A Business Lawyer, Research No. 21,Institute For Career Research, Chicago, 2002

Career As A Criminal Lawyer, Research No. 110, Institute For Career Research, Chicago, 2002

Career As A Tax Attorney, Research Number 207, Institute For Career Research, Chicago, 2001

Career As A Lawyer, Intellectual Property, Research No. 253, Institute For Career Research, Chicago, 1999

Career As A Lawyer, Employment Workplace Law, Research No. 327, Institute For Career Research, Chicago, 2003

Hot Tips From the Experts, Great Ideas for Improving Your Family Law Practice, American Bar Association, 1988